TRAFFIC-FREE
CYCLE TRAILS
SOUTH EAST ENGLAND

NICK COTTON &
KATHY ROGERS

Vertebrate Publishing, Sheffield
www.adventurebooks.com

Traffic-Free Cycle Trails South East England

Traffic-Free Cycle Trails South East England

 Vertebrate Publishing, Omega Court,
352 Cemetery Road, Sheffield S11 8FT.
www.adventurebooks.com

Copyright © Nick Cotton and Vertebrate Publishing 2022.

Front cover: Near the Egrets Way, Sussex. Photo: Simon Eldon Photography.

Back cover: Newport to Sandown on the Isle of Wight; the Egrets Way from Monk's House to Newhaven © SDNPA/AndrewPickettPhoto; Hayling Billy Cycle Trail © Sue Underwood; Cycle Hayling and the Basingstoke Canal from Mytchett Visitor Centre to Byfleet.

Photography by Nick Cotton unless otherwise credited.

Nick Cotton and Kathy Rogers have asserted their rights under the Copyright, Designs and Patents Act 1988 to be identified as authors of this work.

A CIP catalogue record for this book is available from the British Library.

ISBN 978-1-83981-164-7 (Paperback)
ISBN 978-1-83981-165-4 (Ebook)

10 9 8 7 6 5 4 3 2 1

All rights reserved. No part of this work covered by the copyright herein may be reproduced or used in any form or by any means – graphic, electronic, or mechanised, including photocopying, recording, taping or information storage and retrieval systems – without the written permission of the publisher.

Every effort has been made to obtain the necessary permissions with reference to copyright material, both illustrative and quoted. We apologise for any omissions in this respect and will be pleased to make the appropriate acknowledgements in any future edition.

 All maps reproduced by permission of Ordnance Survey on behalf of The Controller of Her Majesty's Stationery Office. © Crown Copyright.

Edited by Jess McElhattan; cover design, layout and production by Rosie Edwards, Vertebrate Publishing.
www.adventurebooks.com

Vertebrate Publishing is committed to printing on paper from sustainable sources.

Printed and bound in Europe by Latitude Press.

TRAFFIC-FREE CYCLE TRAILS

While every attempt has been made to include the vast majority of traffic-free cycle trails in South East England, there will inevitably be omissions. We apologise if we have missed your favourite ride. Please tell us if this is the case, letting us know details of start and finish and cafes and pubs along the way, and we'll try to include it next time. Likewise, if you know of any other routes not listed in this edition of *Traffic-Free Cycle Trails South East England* please contact Nick Cotton, c/o Vertebrate Publishing at the address listed, or email *info@adventurebooks.com*

Contents

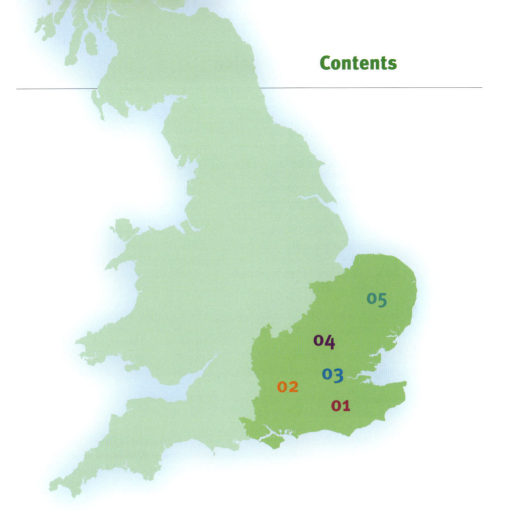

How to use this guide	4	**01 Southern Counties**	20
Useful information	6	**02 Western Counties**	48
Finding a grid reference	7	**03 Greater London**	78
Bike types	9	**04 North of London**	104
Tyres	10	**05 Eastern Counties**	142
Forestry	11		
Mountain biking	14	**Index**	174
National Cycle Network	16		
Other routes in brief	18		

How to use this guide

How do I find a trail near me?
The South East has been divided into five regions, each with a map showing all the trails in the area. So simply look at the map then look up the numbers of the trails nearest to you. Under the entry for each ride number, you will find details of starting point, distance, refreshments, maps and websites. Information about bike hire, shops, public transport and parking is also provided.

What if I know the name of a trail but don't know where it is?
The index at the back will help you to find the Hayling Billy Cycle Trail, Wandle Trail or Downs Link, for example. Then look up the entry.

How do I get to the start of the ride?
We have included details of the closest railway station and of convenient car parking places (including grid references). A grid reference pinpoints on an Ordnance Survey map exactly where a trail starts. To find out how to use these, see p7. Most buses in the UK will not transport bicycles; some coach companies do, but it is space dependent and often requires a bike bag or similar. Most trains will carry bicycles, but space is often very limited (sometimes only two bikes per train); arrangements are different on different trains, even on the same route, and pre-booking is often essential.

What sort of bike should I use?
Each trail description provides information on the trail type, and if a trail is particularly suited to a type of bike, this is mentioned in the introduction. A few are suitable for any bike type. Many are ideal for gravel or hybrid bikes. A small number of the trails are out-and-out mountain bike rides and may get quite muddy in winter. Be prepared for this, or enjoy them after a dry spell in summer. Children's bikes are normally built to withstand knocks and will cope with many of the easier trails.

Do I need special clothes?
Ordinary clothes are fine for all the easier rides. Waterproofs are always useful, and gloves and a hat will stop your hands and

How to use this guide

ears getting cold (a common problem on a bike). If you discover you really love cycling, it is worth investing in cycling shorts and padded gloves, which make riding more comfortable. A top made of 'wicking' fabric will help prevent you getting too clammy.

What should I take with me?
These are short rides and generally not remote, so you do not need to ride with a lot of kit. We would recommend taking a first aid kit, tyre levers, a spare inner tube and puncture repair kit, a chain tool, a multitool, a bike pump, snacks and water. A cable lock and D-lock are useful, and it is worth considering bike lights, particularly in winter. Cable ties and bungee cords are versatile; wrap a short length of gaffer tape around your water bottle for emergency repairs.

How long will each trail take to ride?
We have deliberately avoided giving a time as there are so many variables, the most important of which is YOU! A ride that takes a fit cyclist half an hour could take all day with a group of children. Other variables are the quality of the surface, hills, wind and type of bike. These rides are for enjoyment! Indeed, many of the trails are shared with walkers and horse riders, and you should slow down when there are other users around. Most people of average fitness should cover five to nine miles in an hour, discounting any stops (this type of cycling is two or three times as fast as walking).

Are all the rides 100 per cent traffic-free?
Most of the trails have long sections of traffic-free cycling but, inevitably, many have to cross roads, and some routes also use quiet lanes. You are given a warning if there are any busier roads to cross.

Will I find somewhere to eat?
If there is a convenient pub, tea room or cafe along the trail then we have mentioned it. Forestry routes and trails around National Trust estates or country parks often start at a visitor centre where you can usually buy hot drinks and light meals, or at least snacks. It is always worth carrying a bar of something and a bottle of water, particularly when riding with children.

What if I break down?
None of these rides are so long or remote that you couldn't walk back to the start or somewhere where your bike can be fixed. The usual problem is a puncture, so carry a spare tube and a pump. Multitools, with screwdrivers, Allen keys and spanners can be used to tighten up nuts, bolts and screws that rattle loose, and can adjust saddle height. Many cycle hire companies offer a repair or rescue service as part of the rental.

In an emergency, you should call 999. In Great Britain, the emergency services can also be contacted by SMS text – useful if you have low battery or intermittent signal. Although primarily aimed at deaf and speech impaired people, EmergencySMS is available to anyone, if your service provider supports it, but it requires registration; you can register by sending an SMS message, 'register' to 999 (the UK) or 112 (Ireland). It is particularly useful in areas of the countryside where mobile signal is too

Useful information

weak to sustain phone contact but a text message might be sent. **EmergencySMS should only be used when voice call contact with emergency services is not possible.**

Does the book include trails on the National Cycle Network?
The National Cycle Network (NCN) is a mixture of cycle lanes, quiet streets, country lanes and traffic-free trails. Many NCN traffic-free sections over three miles are included. You will know you are on the National Cycle Network by the red and white route number signs. You will find a section on the National Cycle Network (p16), listing the maps that cover the area. These maps highlight all traffic-free sections and – who knows? – you may be tempted to do an entire long-distance route, such as the famous South Downs Way from Winchester to Eastbourne. Bear in mind that the National Cycle Network often updates its routes, which may impact the title, cover or routes in the maps mentioned. The best place to find the most up-to-date information is the Sustrans website – *www.sustrans.org.uk*

What about mountain biking?
Most of the forestry rides are tougher than railway paths and some areas have purpose-built singletrack mountain bike trails. There are also long-distance trails such as the Ridgeway, South Downs Way or Peddars Way, which are more of a challenge. This introduction includes a map with details of good mountain biking areas or centres (p15). Most good bookshops will stock a range of cycling guides, including ones covering mountain biking, and there is a lot of information on the internet – we have listed useful websites (p19).

Where else can I ride, traffic-free and legally?
You have a right to ride on bridleways and byways, all shown on Ordnance Survey maps, but these are a bit hit and miss in terms of quality. You are NOT allowed to ride on footpaths. The majority of canal towpaths are too narrow, rough, muddy or overgrown to be much fun. The best option is to go to the nearest public-owned forestry holding where you can explore the broad stone tracks (forestry operations permitting). There is a map of the forestry holdings at the start of the book (p13). What used to be the Forestry Commission has now spilt into three: Forestry England, Forestry and Land Scotland, and Natural Resources Wales. In England, you may not cycle on open access land (except on bridleways and byways, or if permission is granted by the landowner).

What about riding on lanes?
After you have built up your confidence there is no reason why you should not explore Britain's fantastic network of quiet country lanes by bike. In this introduction there are details of good areas with suggested bases from which to start. Many of the waymarked long-distance routes on the National Cycle Network are also good options for longer rides.

Useful information

Finding a grid reference
What is a grid reference?
A grid reference is a number that allows you to pinpoint a place on a map. It looks and sounds technical, but is easy to learn. Grid references can be enormously helpful, saving the need for heaps of directions you would otherwise require.

Why is it called a grid reference?
If you look at any Ordnance Survey map there are numbered blue lines running across and down the map – these form a grid. In the case of the Landranger maps, which we refer to a lot in this book, there are 40 vertical and 40 horizontal lines, creating 1,600 squares on each map, each of which represents one square kilometre (just over half a mile by half a mile). There are fewer but bigger squares on Explorer maps, but each one also represents one square kilometre.

So how does it work?
There are times when you want to direct people to a point in one of the squares formed by the grid to find a feature (a pub, a railway station, etc.) contained in that square. Within the six-figure grid reference, the first set of three numbers gives you an imaginary line running up and down the map (south–north), the last set of three numbers gives you a line running across the map (west–east). Where these imaginary lines cross is the place on the map you want to pinpoint.

How do you work out the first three figures of a grid reference?
The first two numbers of the six-figure grid reference refer to the vertical line on the left of the chosen square. These double-digit numbers can be found along the top and bottom edges of the map. For the third number in the series, imagine the chosen square, the one to the right of the vertical line, divided into ten vertical strips, numbered from '1' on the left to '9' on the right. The third number locates one of these strips so, for example, '2' would be towards the left of the square and '8' would be towards the right.

What about the last three numbers?
These refer to the horizontal lines. Instead of starting at the left of the chosen square, start from the bottom and work towards the top. (To find the numbers, look at the left- or right-hand edges of the map.) The line at the bottom of the chosen square gives you the fourth and fifth numbers in the six-figure grid reference.

To calculate the sixth number, imagine the chosen square above the horizontal line split into ten horizontal strips, numbered from '1' at the bottom to '9' at the top. The sixth and final number of the six-figure grid reference locates one of these strips. For example, '2' would be towards the bottom of the square and '8' would be towards the top.

Put the vertical numbers together with the horizontal and you have a six-figure grid reference, and can locate a point on the map to a high degree of accuracy. To help you remember which set of numbers goes first, always remember the saying 'along the corridor and up the stairs' – i.e. work along the map from left to right, then up the map from bottom to top.

Useful information

The Towpath Code

1. Share the space
Towpaths are popular places to be enjoyed by everyone. Please be mindful of others. Keep dogs under control and clean up after them.

2. Drop your pace
Pedestrians have priority on towpaths so cyclists need to be ready to slow down. If you're in a hurry, consider using an alternative route for your journey.

3. It's a special place
Waterways are living history with boats, working locks and low bridges, so please give way to waterway users and be extra careful where visibility is limited.

For more information about towpath cycling, visit: canalrivertrust.org.uk/enjoy-the-waterways/cycling

The Forest Cycle Code

Before you travel
- Don't rely on others.
- Ensure you can get home safely.
- Carry the right equipment and know how to use it.

For your safety
- Wear the right safety clothing: a helmet and gloves.
- Cycle within your abilities.
- Look first: only tackle jumps and other challenges if you are sure you can do them.
- Train properly, especially for difficult and technical routes.

On- and off-road
- Expect the unexpected: watch out for other visitors.
- Stay safe: always follow warning signs and other information you are given.
- If a vehicle is loading timber, always wait for the driver to let you past.

In an emergency, dial 999. Once you are safe, please let the local forest centre know by telephone.

For more information about forest cycling, go to: www.forestryengland.uk/cycling

KEY

- 🚉 Public transport
- 🅿 Parking
- ✕ Refreshments
- WC Toilets
- £ Bike hire
- ⌁ Challenging riding

Useful information

Bike types

Road	Road bikes have a lightweight frame, dropped handlebars and slick, or smooth, tyres and are designed to be ridden at speed over tarmacked or paved surfaces. Road cyclists often cycle in a crouch position using the bottom of the drop handlebars.
Touring	Touring bikes are similar to road bikes, but are designed to cover long distances on the road. They have a frame strong enough to withstand luggage carrying, and adaptations such as luggage mounts and mudguards. They have a longer wheelbase (the horizontal distance between front and back wheels) than road bikes.
Hybrid	Hybrid bikes are a blend of road and mountain bike and are designed to tolerate riding over a wide range of terrains and in different weather conditions. They tend to have the mountain bike's flat handlebars and upright cycling position but the narrower wheels of a road bike and luggage mounts of a touring bike.
Gravel	Gravel bikes are a road/mountain bike hybrid, designed to facilitate long-distance riding over varied terrains, both on- and off-road. They usually have drop handlebars, a road-style frame but wider, knobblier tyres and a longer wheelbase, and the front wheel is further forward to provide better stability. They have much wider tyre clearance than road or hybrid bikes.
Mountain	Mountain bikes are designed to ride over rough terrain, and generally have wider, stronger wheels with knobbly tyres, flat handlebars and up to 27 gears. They may have suspension on both the front and back wheels (full suspension), front suspension (a 'hardtail'), or no suspension (rigid). Fat tyres are all-terrain bikes with extremely wide, often low-inflated, tyres (in excess of 3.8 inches/97mm). You generally cycle in an upright position on a mountain bike.
Ebike	Any type of bike can be an e- or electric bike. An ebike has a battery and a motor; ebikes are either pedal assist (they provide power when the pedals are turned) or power on demand (controlled by a throttle). Ebikes can be ridden without a licence or registration but the UK places restrictions on the maximum speed and motor power on ebikes. An ebike can be a good choice for a longer cycle trail as they 'flatten' the hills, compensate for riding with heavy loads and can enable longer distances. However, particularly with off-road routes, it may be hard to find recharging points and ebikes are heavier than their conventional equivalents, limit your luggage-carrying options and are more difficult to pedal with a dead battery.
Other	Tandem bikes are built for two or more people, and recumbent bicycles are ridden in a laid-back rather than seated position. Tricycles have a pair of wheels (usually at the back) and a single wheel, and unicycles have a saddle above a single wheel. Handcycles are cycles, usually tricycles, powered by movement of the arms and hands rather than legs and feet.

Useful information

Tyres

One simple adaptation you can make to your bike to improve your trail experience is to choose the right tyres for your ride.

Width – tyre widths range from 20mm (road tyres) to 100mm (fat tyres). Although the width of your wheel and tyre will be constrained by your bike choice, even a few extra millimetres on a road tyre can make your bike more stable, while a slightly narrower mountain bike tyre will help you make faster progress on tarmac sections.

Tread – switching slick road tyres for those with slightly more grip will give you more stability on a bicycle. Consider the best tread for mountain bike tyres based on what types of surface you will encounter on the trail, the time of year (in winter it is usually muddier) and weather conditions you will face and how far you will travel on hard surfaces.

Tubeless – most wheels use a thin rubber inner tube, filled with air, and a thicker outer tyre. Tubeless tyres seal under the wheel rim to provide an air cushion with no need for an inner tube. Tubeless tyres are less susceptible to flat tyres, as this is generally a result of punctures to the inner tube, and small holes in tubeless tyres can be sealed with liquid sealant. Tubeless tyres can also be ridden at lower pressures than conventional tyres, which offers better traction over rough terrain. Tubeless tyres are difficult to repair when they do acquire a large puncture and can be heavier than tyre and inner-tube combinations.

Cycling organisations

Sustrans (www.sustrans.org.uk) is a charity formed in 1977, whose aim is to create and promote better walking and cycling routes. It is the custodian of the National Cycle Network.

Cycling UK (cyclinguk.org) is a charitable membership organisation, founded in 1878 and formerly known as the Cyclists' Touring Club. It promotes and enables cycling for everybody by promoting flagship routes, organising local events and rides, offering practical support to cyclists and lobbying for safer cycling environments.

British Cycling (www.britishcycling.org.uk) is the sports governing body for most competitive cycling in the UK. It also promotes leisure cycling, through initiatives such as Breeze and Let's Ride.

The **National Cycle Network** (NCN) is a signposted network of national cycle trails, developed by Sustrans, since the 1980s. The network consisted of waymarked routes on well-maintained, well-surfaced paths and trails and roads. However, Sustrans reviewed the network in 2018 and removed or reclassified approximately a quarter of its 25,000-kilometre network. It is in the process of removing all signage from 1,200 kilometres of road that once formed part of the network but are now deemed too busy or dangerous to form part of the network.

Forestry

For such a densely populated area, the south-east of England has, surprisingly, more woodland than either the South West or the Midlands. The largest forestry holding is the New Forest but there are also large swathes of woodland along the South Downs. North of London, there is a small, densely forested centre on the sandy soils around Thetford, and two reasonable-sized holdings (Tunstall and Rendlesham) to the north-east of Ipswich, near the Suffolk coast. The Forestry England website (*www.forestryengland.uk/cycling*) is a good starting point to find places to ride.

see *www.forestryengland.uk/forest-planning* or *www.forestryengland.uk/search-forests* for an A–Z list of England's forests.

© CHRIS COLES

Forests and woods with waymarked trails
The New Forest (shown as 2 on the map overleaf)
Although this is by far the largest forest in the South East, there is no set list of waymarked circular rides; instead, you will find a large network of excellent, broad, gravel-based trails waymarked with green and white disks that enable you to make up your own rides. Key to this is the map produced by Forestry England called New Forest Cycle Routes Map.

Forestry England woodlands
There are other woodlands owned by Forestry England where there are no waymarked routes, but you are free to explore the tracks as long as it is safe to do so (i.e. no tree harvesting is taking place).

The relevant Ordnance Survey map is mentioned. It is highly recommended that you take a map or a phone with mapping loaded on it for the larger woods as it is very easy to get lost. To find the location of these woodlands

Forestry

These woodlands are shown on Ordnance Survey Landranger mapping (1:50,000) with a purple highlight around the boundary of the forestry holding and a purple small square icon with two trees. There is nothing to distinguish Forestry England woods from other woods on Ordnance Survey Explorer mapping (1:25,000); the woods are depicted without a symbol but with a pale orange border.

The following woodlands correspond with the numbers on the map:

1. **Brighstone & Parkhurst Forests**, Isle of Wight (OS Explorer Map OL29)

2. **New Forest**, Hampshire (OS Explorer Map OL22, p53)

3. **Farley Mount**, west of Winchester (OS Explorer Map 132)

4. **West Walk**, north of Fareham (OS Explorer Map 119)

5. **Queen Elizabeth Country Park**, Petersfield (OS Explorer Map OL33, p56)

6. **Alice Holt Forest**, Farnham (OS Explorer Maps 144 & 145, p63)

7. **Charlton Forest & Eartham Wood**, south-east of Midhurst (OS Explorer Map 121)

8. **Rewell Wood**, west of Arundel (OS Explorer Map 121)

9. **Friston Forest**, Eastbourne (OS Explorer Map OL25, p32)

10. **Wilmington Wood & Abbot's Wood**, south-west of Hailsham (OS Explorer Map 123)

11. **Bedgebury Forest**, Hawkhurst (OS Explorer Map 136, p39)

12. **Hemsted Forest**, east of Cranbrook (OS Explorer Maps 125 & 137)

13. **King's Wood**, north of Ashford (OS Explorer Map 137)

14. **West Wood**, Elhampark & Covert Wood, east of Ashford (OS Explorer Map 138)

15. **Denge Wood**, north-east of Ashford (OS Explorer Map 137)

16. **Clowes Wood**, north of Canterbury (OS Explorer Map 150)

17. **Shabbington Wood & Waterperry Wood**, east of Oxford (OS Explorer Map 180)

18. **Wendover Woods**, Aylesbury (OS Explorer Map 181, p107)

19. **Rendlesham Forest**, north-east of Ipswich (OS Explorer Maps 197 & 212, p158)

20. **King's Forest & Mildenhall Woods**, south-west of Thetford (OS Explorer Maps 226 & 229)

21. **Thetford Forest**, north-west of Thetford (OS Explorer Map 229, p163)

22. **West Harling Heath**, east of Thetford (OS Explorer Map 230)

Forestry

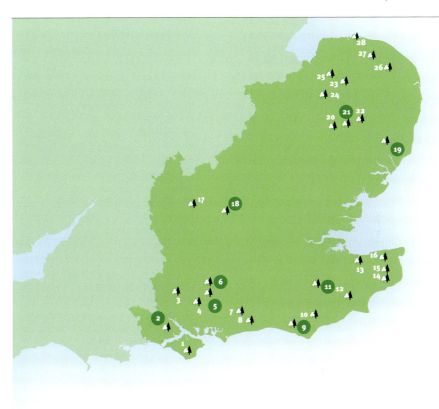

23. **Swaffham Heath & Cockleycley Heath**, south-east of Swaffham (OS Explorer Map 236)

24. **Coldharbour Wood & Shakers Wood**, south of Swaffham (OS Explorer Maps 229 & 236)

25. **Shouldham Warren/The Sincks**, south of King's Lynn (OS Explorer Map 236)

26. **Horsford Woods**, north of Norwich (OS Explorer Map 238)

27. **Swanton Great Wood**, east of Fakenham (OS Explorer Map 251)

28. **Woodlands** between Holt and Sheringham (OS Explorer Map 252)

Mountain biking

South of London, mountain biking is almost exclusively on the chalk and flint tracks that abound in the area. These are best enjoyed in the summer months (from May to October) when the trails are drier and easier to ride: they can become impassable in the depths of winter. The main exception to the chalk is the area lying just south of the North Downs, where there are many sandy tracks – often easier when they are wet and harder packed (compare riding on a wet sandy beach or a dry sandy beach). This sandy area extends east from Alton in Hampshire across towards Dorking, Reigate and Oxted in Surrey, and on to Maidstone and Ashford in Kent.

To the north of London, there are several mountain biking options including Thetford Forest (p163), the Suffolk coast forests (p158), Epping Forest (p100) and rides along the Icknield Way (p108) and Peddars Way (p172). The latter is a long-distance trail that runs as a byway or bridleway for around 50 miles from Lackford, south-west of Thetford, to the north Norfolk coast at Holme next the Sea. Although maps show that there are plenty of bridleways and byways in Essex and Hertfordshire, these are predominantly very rough and very muddy in the winter, and baked hard into bumpy corrugations in the summer.

For forest trails, see the South East forestry section (p11) and visit the Forestry England website.

1. Isle of Wight
There are many miles of excellent tracks on the Isle of Wight, particularly the Tennyson Trail (p50) on the western half of the island between Freshwater Bay and Newport.

2. Hampshire Downs
As with Wiltshire and Dorset, Hampshire is blessed with many hundreds of miles of chalk and flint byways and bridleways. Some of the waymarked long-distance trails (such as the Wayfarer's Walk and the Test Way, both of which start on Inkpen Hill to the south of Hungerford) have long bridleway and byway sections. Winchester is also the start of the South Downs Way, one of the premier long-distance bridleways in the country that runs east for 100 miles to Eastbourne.

3. King Alfred's Way
King Alfred's Way is a 220-mile, circular, off-road adventure route, launched by Cycling UK in 2020. It includes sections of the Ridgeway, South Downs Way and Thames Path and takes in Stonehenge, Winchester and the Devil's Punch Bowl. There are occasional road sections, but it generally follows off-road trails best suited to gravel or mountain bikes.

4. Berkshire Downs (Ridgeway)
There is a plethora of fine tracks to the south of the Ridgeway and to the north of the M4 through west Berkshire and south Oxfordshire. Lambourn is an excellent base with tracks radiating off in every direction.

5. Chiltern Hills
The beechwoods of the Chilterns offer splendid woodland rides on well-maintained and well-waymarked bridleways and byways. The best tracks lie to the west and north of Henley-on-Thames.

6. North Downs
Unlike the South Downs Way or the Ridgeway, where you are allowed to cycle from one end to the other, the

Mountain biking

North Downs Way – running along the chalk ridge from Farnham to Canterbury and Dover – is mainly a footpath (you are not permitted to cycle on footpaths). There are, however, several long bridleway and byway sections that are open to cyclists, easily found by looking at the relevant Ordnance Survey map. There are many good bases from which to explore the North Downs bridleway and byway network: Gomshall, Peaslake, Leith Hill, Walton on the Hill, Limpsfield and Wye.

7. South Downs
The South Downs Way is a 100-mile linear bridleway from Winchester to Eastbourne. A few miles either side of the trail there are many other bridleways and byways, enabling you to devise all sorts of circular rides. The South Downs tracks are very definitely best ridden in summer after a few dry days; the chalk and clay can be depressingly sticky in winter.

8. Icknield Way
The Icknield Way Path is part of the Greater Ridgeway footpath, an ancient route that runs across England from Dorset to Norfolk. As some of the trail cannot be cycled, an alternative Icknield Way Trail route for horse riders and cyclists has been created; this sometimes follows roads where there is no off-road alternative. It is a challenging route, but is a good starting point for those looking for off-road routes between Buckinghamshire and Norfolk. It connects with the Peddars Way.

15

National Cycle Network

The following long-distance National Cycle Network routes are covered by maps that can be purchased from Sustrans via their shop (*www.sustrans.org.uk*). Bear in mind that the National Cycle Network routes are often updated, which may impact the title, cover or routes in the maps mentioned here. The best place to find the most up-to-date information is the Sustrans website.

The Varsity Way Cycle Route Map
(Route 12/51) Oxford to Cambridge
– 124 miles

London to Brighton Cycle Route Map
(Route 21/20) – 58 miles

Shakespeare Cycleway Cycle Route Map
(Route 4/5) Stratford-upon-Avon to London – 167 miles

South Coast East Cycle Route Map
(Route 2) Brockenhurst to Dover
– 178 miles

Great Western Way Cycle Route Map
(Route 4) Bristol to London
– 167 miles

The National Cycle Network in the south-east of England is covered by the following maps:
6. Hampshire & Isle of Wight Cycle Map
7. Central Sussex & South Surrey Cycle Map
8. Kent Cycle Map
9. Essex & Thames Estuary Cycle Map
10. Thames Valley Cycle Map
17. South Cambridgeshire, Bedfordshire & North Hertfordshire Cycle Map
18. Suffolk Cycle Map
19. Norfolk Cycle Map
20. The Fens Cycle Map
53. London Cycle Map

National Cycle Network

Good areas for lane cycling

From a cyclist's point of view, much of the South East has a high population density and high levels of car ownership, filling many of the roads with traffic. The concept of 'quiet lane networks' is somewhat alien in this region. The best rule of thumb is that the further away you go from London, the quieter the roads will become – for example, try **west** or **north Oxfordshire** with good bases at Burford or Hook Norton; **north Buckinghamshire** from **Winslow** or **Buckingham**; **south Hampshire** has networks of lanes between the M3 and the A3; in the **eastern half of Kent** it is worth exploring lanes **south-west**, **south** and **south-east of Canterbury**.

East Anglia has hundreds of miles of quiet lanes with gentle gradients linking small villages. As the weather tends to be much drier here than on the west side of the country, you have a set of excellent conditions for enjoyable cycling for day rides or longer touring. The southern part of the region is fairly densely populated but there is a lot less traffic north of an imaginary line drawn from Luton to Colchester – i.e. **north Essex, Suffolk and Norfolk**.

There are many attractive villages that would make good bases in Norfolk, such as Castle Acre, Little Walsingham, Burnham Market, Reepham or Aylsham. Elsewhere, Thaxted in Essex or Lavenham, Framlingham and Beccles in Suffolk are all wonderful bases around which there is a delightful network of lanes to explore.

Other routes in brief

The best starting place to discover the latest information about cycling infrastructure is usually the main council website, for example, in Norfolk, go to *www.norfolk.gov.uk* and search for 'Cycle routes' or 'Cycling'. In popular tourist areas, there is often a tourist-orientated website which may provide useful information on leisure cycling routes (for example, *www.visitisleofwight.co.uk*).

Bedfordshire
Try this website for cycling information in and around Bedford: *www.travelbedford.co.uk* and click on 'Cycling' then 'Maps & Routes'.

Berkshire
Maps are available to download on this website: *www.westberks.gov.uk* and search 'Cycling'.

Cambridgeshire
There is a series of useful maps to download on the county council website. Go to *www.cambridgeshire.gov.uk* and search 'Cycle maps'.

East Sussex
The council website is a useful starting point to find rides in the area. Go to *www.eastsussex.gov.uk* and search 'Cycling maps'.

Essex
The county council website is a good source of information: *www.essexhighways.org/getting-around/cycling.aspx*

Hampshire
Details of 750 miles of off-road cycle routes and urban cycle paths can be found at *www.hants.gov.uk/thingstodo/countryside/cycling* or *www.visit-hampshire.co.uk/cycling/cycle-routes* and click on 'Car free trails'.

Hertfordshire
Try the county council website for cycling ideas: *www.hertfordshire.gov.uk* and search 'Cycling routes'.

Isle of Wight
A good website to get an overview of cycling possibilities on the island is: *www.visitisleofwight.co.uk/things-to-do/cycling*

Other routes in brief

Kent
The 'Explore Kent' website is a good place to start for ride ideas: www.explorekent.org/activities or try www.visitkent.co.uk/see-and-do/active-and-outdoors/cycling

London
There is a lot of useful information about cycling in the capital on the Transport for London website: tfl.gov.uk/modes/cycling/

New Forest National Park
There are plenty of ride suggestions on the national park's website. Go to www.newforestnpa.gov.uk/todo/cycling

Oxfordshire
For routes and maps in and around Oxford go to www.oxford.gov.uk and search 'Cycling routes'.

South Downs National Park
There are many ideas for cycle rides on the national park's website. Go to www.southdowns.gov.uk/enjoy/cycling and click on 'Cycle routes'.

Suffolk
Try the county council website for cycling information – go to www.discoversuffolk.org.uk and search 'Cycling'. Try also www.suffolkonboard.com/cycle

Surrey
For ride suggestions in Surrey and useful maps you can download, go to www.surreycc.gov.uk and search 'Cycling routes'.

West Sussex
For a cycling overview go to www.westsussex.gov.uk and search 'Cycling maps'.

Other useful websites with cycling information
- www.canalrivertrust.org.uk
- www.nationaltrust.org.uk/cycling
- www.sustrans.org.uk/national-cycle-network
- www.forestryengland.uk/cycling
- www.moredirt.com
- www.trailforks.com
- www.komoot.com
- www.essexhertsmtb.co.uk
- www.surreyhillsmountainbiking.co.uk
- www.visit-hampshire.co.uk/cycling/cycling-types/mountain-biking
- www.b1ke.com/b1keparks/rogate

© CHRIS COLES

TRAFFIC-FREE CYCLE TRAILS SOUTH EAST ENGLAND

Southern Counties

1. Centurion Way, Chichester
2. Wey Navigation: Guildford to Godalming
3. The Hurtwood
4. Downs Link: Bramley to Cranleigh
5. Downs Link: Cranleigh south to Slinfold
6. Downs Link: Southwater to Bramber
7. Downs Link: Bramber to Old Shoreham
8. Brighton Promenade
9. Ditchling Beacon on the South Downs Way
10. Egrets Way: Monk's House to Newhaven
11. Friston Forest
12. Cuckoo Trail
13. Deers Leap Park

Southern Counties

01

Southern Counties

Southern Counties

14 Worth Way, west of East Grinstead
15 Forest Way, east of East Grinstead
16 Tudor Trail: Tonbridge to Penshurst Place
17 Bewl Water, Lamberhurst
18 Bedgebury Forest
19 Rye Harbour Nature Reserve Loop
20 The Medway Towpath
21 North Downs Way: Lenham to Charing
22 Hythe Seafront
23 The Great Stour Way
24 Crab and Winkle Way: Canterbury to Whitstable
25 The Oyster Bay Trail: Whitstable to Hampton Pier
26 The Viking Coastal Trail: Reculver to Margate

© CONTAINS ORDNANCE SURVEY DATA © CROWN COPYRIGHT AND DATABASE RIGHT

Ride 1 Centurion Way Chichester

Start
Junction of Park Lane and A286, West Dean (50.9035, -0.7833, SU 856123)

Finish
Westgate, Chichester (50.8360, -0.7969, SU 848047)

Distance
6 miles/10km.

Category
Railway paths.

Other facilities

The railway path between Chichester and West Dean passes some extraordinary metal sculptures of Roman centurions and 'surveyors'. The route runs through woodland and arable land with a profusion of wildflowers along the verges. The name Centurion Way was suggested by a local schoolboy and is based on the fact that the path crosses the course of a Roman road. From the southern end of the path it is easy to visit Chichester Cathedral, to link to a short section of the Chichester Canal towpath or to the longer route known as the Salterns Way, which is a mixture of quiet lanes and traffic-free sections. The Chichester to Midhurst railway was opened in 1881 and was finally closed in 1991. In 1994 the county council purchased the railway line and the old railway line was converted to recreational use.

Refreshments: The Selsey Arms pub and tea room at Village Store in West Dean; the Earl of March pub in Mid Lavant. Lots of choice in Chichester.
Bike hire and repairs: Spares and repairs from BIKEsquared, Barreg Cycles, Hargrove Cycles, Geared Bikes in Chichester.
Public transport and bike links: Fishbourne and Chichester stations, 1 mile from end. National Cycle Network (NCN) Route 2 (which links Kent to Cornwall) passes through Chichester.
Parking: Limited free on-road parking in West Dean and near end in Chichester.
Maps and guides: OS Landranger 197, Explorer OL8.
Website: www.westsussex.gov.uk/leisure-recreation-and-community/walking-horse-riding-and-cycling/centurion-way-railway-path/

On your bikes!
From West Dean, heading south
1. Turn left on to the cycle path alongside the main A286 road. After 1 mile, at the end of the cycle path, with a red letter box set in a brick wall ahead, turn left downhill on a rough track, soon joining the railway path running along the valley.

2. At the houses in Mid Lavant, aim for the far-right-hand corner of the 'green' then turn left. Continue in the same direction, ignoring turns to the left. Pass between concrete bollards and as the road swings right, bear left on to Churchmead Close, signposted 'Chichester'. Take the next left on Warble Heath Close, signposted 'Chichester', to rejoin the railway path for a gentle descent over almost 3 miles to Chichester. You may wish to turn around at the end of the traffic-free section, but if you want to go into the centre of Chichester, turn left and follow Westgate and West Street to the cathedral.

SOUTHERN COUNTIES

Wey Navigation: Godalming to Guildford
Ride 2

Two sections of the Wey Navigation are suitable for cycling – both are described in this guide (see also p82). The canal was part of a series of waterways connecting London to Portsmouth via the River Arun and Chichester Harbour. Barges transported large quantities of government stores and ammunition to Godalming, from where it was taken on to the naval arsenal at Portsmouth. The 1830s were the highpoint of the waterways, when tonnage carried was at its highest. Competition from the railways began to take away trade from the waterways from the 1840s onwards. The quality of the towpath is variable and mountain or gravel bikes are recommended. It is easy to link this ride to the Downs Link at a point close to where the railway crosses the canal to the west of Shalford. Look out for the extraordinary cliffs of yellow sand at the northern end of the trail.

On your bikes!

1. From the south end of Millmead in Guildford (by the council offices and the Britannia pub), cross the river into the park and follow the path alongside the Wey Navigation, keeping the water to your left, soon passing the Guildford Rowing Club.

2. The quality of the towpath varies. After about 1.5 miles, pass under a railway bridge.

If you wish to join the Downs Link, about 100m after the railway bridge keep an eye out for an old World War II pillbox up to your right. This is the start of the Downs Link. The surface quality improves after about $1/2$ mile.

3. Stay on the towpath and cross the busy A248 (**take care**), then after a further mile cross the next road by Farncombe Boat House and Hector's on the Wey.

4. The towpath ends near the Godalming United Church just north of the bridge over the river in Godalming.

Refreshments: Lots of choice in Guildford. Hector's on the Wey cafe at Farncombe. Lots of choice in Godalming.
Bike hire and repairs: Electric bike hire from Electric Bikes Guildford; several bike shops in Guildford.
Public transport and bike links: Guildford station, $1/2$ mile from start. Godalming station, $1/2$ mile from end.
Parking: Millmead car park at start. Paid car parks in Godalming town centre.
Maps and guides: OS Landranger 186, Explorer 145.
Website: www.nationaltrust.org.uk/river-wey-and-godalming-navigations-and-dapdune-wharf

Start
Britannia pub, Guildford (51.2331, -0.5758, SU 995492)

Finish
Godalming United Church, Godalming (51.1882 -0.6082, SU 973441)

Distance
4.5 miles/7.5km.

Category
Canal towpaths.

Other facilities

Ride 3 The Hurtwood

Start/finish
YHA Holmbury St Mary Surrey Hills, Dorking (51.1935, -0.4214, TQ 104450)

Distance
3 miles/5km.

Category
Forestry trails.

Other facilities

The Hurtwood is a woodland area of common land in Surrey; in 1926 local mayor Reggie Bray signed a deed of dedication, granting public access to the land for 'quiet enjoyment'. With its towering Scots pines, purpled heathland and cloudy ponds, the woods offer some of the best off-road cycle trails in Surrey. Such is the proliferation of trails through the Hurtwood and its neighbouring woodlands that it is possible for the enthusiastic endurance cyclist to ride from Guildford to Dorking off-road. The route described below is a shorter loop around the Hurtwood; there are miles and miles more of trails and bridleways to explore.

On your bikes!

1. Enter the woods via Telegraph Road; just behind the car park, turn right. At a junction of 3 tracks, take the left trail to enter the woods rather than continuing around the edge. The trail now climbs.

2. Go straight across the first crossroads (after 400m); after 500m, turn right at another track crossroads – ignore the fifth track forking right from the crossroads.

3. Turn right near the car park. You can follow this new bridleway for 500m to reach the viewpoint at the top of Holmbury Hill; there is also a hill fort at the summit. If you take this detour, you will have to retrace your steps. If you do not choose to climb Holmbury Hill, turn almost immediately left. After 400m, take the right fork.

4. At the track crossroads, you can continue straight on if you wish to visit

Refreshments: Hurtwood Cafe at youth hostel at start. Pub and cafe at Holmbury St Mary, slight detour from route.
Bike hire and repairs: Hire from Surrey Hills Mountain Biking, Peaslake.
Public transport and bike links: Gomshall station, 2.5 miles from start, largely on bridleways.
Parking: Free car park at start.
Maps and guides: OS Landranger 187, Explorer 145 & 146.
Website: *foth.co.uk*

the village of Holmbury St Mary; there is a pub and a cafe. If you want to explore further, this is a good point at which to turn right and then left to remain on the Greensand Way and follow it through the neighbouring woods to Leith Hill Tower. To complete your loop instead, turn left and follow the trail back to the start.

24

SOUTHERN COUNTIES

Downs Link: Ride 4
Bramley to Cranleigh

As its name suggests, this railway path route links the North Downs Way with the South Downs Way. The Downs Link, which is over 30 miles long, has been split into several sections. There is a short one-mile railway path stretch to the north of Bramley, as far as the A281, but the trail described here heads south from Bramley to Cranleigh. This section of the trail is owned and managed by Surrey County Council. Small areas of trees are periodically cut back (coppiced) to diversify the woodland structure and encourage the growth of wildflowers. This also benefits butterflies, small mammals and bird life. The railway was built in two sections: the southern part, from Christ's Hospital to Shoreham-by-Sea, was completed in 1861 and the northern part, from Guildford to Christ's Hospital, was built in 1865. The railways served the local communities and industries like the Southwater Brickworks but were not profitable and were shut in 1966.

On your bikes!

1. Join the bridleway where it crosses Station Road, at the site of the old Bramley and Wonersh station (next to the Bramley Business Centre). It is signed 'NCN 22'; follow the finger post pointing towards Shoreham and Cranleigh.

2. Follow the route for 6 miles until it emerges on John Wiskar Drive in Cranleigh, just behind the High Street. This is a family friendly route as the trail tends to cross under roads.

Refreshments: Pub in Bramley. Lots of choice in Cranleigh.
Bike hire and repairs: Repairs from the Fettling Room (cycling hub and cafe) and Cycle Wizard in Cranleigh; more bike shops in Guildford.
Public transport and bike links: Shalford station, 1.5 miles from start (Downs Link can be followed much of the way).
Parking: Free Bramley and Wonersh station car park, near start. Paid car park off Cranleigh High Street.
Maps and guides: OS Landranger 186 & 187, Explorer OL34.
Website: www.westsussex.gov.uk/leisure-recreation-and-community/walking-horse-riding-and-cycling/downs-link

Start
Station Road, Bramley (51.1960, -0.5559, TQ 010451)

Finish
John Wiskar Drive, Cranleigh (51.1402, -0.4908, TQ 057390)

Distance
6 miles/10km.

Category
Railway paths.

Other facilities

25

Ride 5 Downs Link: Cranleigh south to Slinfold

Start
John Wiskar Drive, Cranleigh (51.1404 -0.4904, TQ 057389)

Finish
Hayes Lane, Slinfold (51.0658, -0.4063, TQ 117308) or Christ's Hospital rail station (51.0507, -0.3637, TQ 147 292)

Distance
7 miles/11.5km to Slinfold; 10 miles/16km to Christ's Hospital.

Category
Railway paths.

Other facilities

It is worth cycling this section in May when the woods south of Baynards are carpeted with a magnificent display of bluebells. The stone-based track will become muddy in winter or after prolonged rain. There is one hill south of Baynards where the trail has to climb up over the blocked tunnel that the railway used to use. There are a couple of minor lanes to cross and one busy road – the A281 south of Rudgwick – where you should take GREAT CARE.

On your bikes!

1. Turn right on to the Downs Link from John Wiskar Drive (by low wooden posts, signposted 'Downs Link'), approximately 25m from its junction with Knowle Lane. Follow the track/lane between playing fields. Continue for 3.5 miles to the old station at Baynards.

2. At a tarmac lane just beyond the old station turn left then right, signposted 'Downs Link'. Go under the first bridge, turn sharp left uphill on to the road, cross the bridge then take the first left through a gate signposted 'Downs Link'. In order to avoid the old tunnel you now have a steep climb. After 350m, at a crossroads of tracks at the top, turn left and go steeply downhill. (**Remember** this point for the return trip.)

3. About 1 mile after rejoining the course of the railway line you have to cross the busy A281. **TAKE GREAT CARE.**

4. After 2 miles, and about 200m after going through a short, round tunnel beneath the A29 and past a factory on your right, turn left by an information board on to tarmac to go into Slinfold. At the T-junction at the end of the lane, turn right for the pub in the village. Alternatively, you can choose to continue on the Downs Link for a further 3 miles to reach Christ's Hospital railway station; this section of the Link was restored in 2020.

Refreshments: Lots of choice in Cranleigh. Red Lyon pub just off route in Slinfold.
Bike hire and repairs: Repairs from the Fettling Room (cycling hub and cafe) and Cycle Wizard in Cranleigh. Mike the Bike's charity bike shop, Slinfold.
Public transport and bike links:
Downs Link can be followed to Christ's Hospital, 3 miles from Slinfold. If tackling by public transport, Downs Link provides almost entirely traffic-free route between Shalford and Christ's Hospital rail stations.
Parking: Paid car park off Cranleigh High Street; limited free on-street parking in Slinfold.
Maps and guides: OS Landranger 187, Explorer OL34.
Website: www.westsussex.gov.uk/leisure-recreation-and-community/walking-horse-riding-and-cycling/downs-link

SOUTHERN COUNTIES

Downs Link: Ride 6
Southwater to Bramber

South from Southwater, the views open up with the whaleback ridge of the South Downs looming on the horizon. One suggested turn-around point is the pub at Partridge Green. If you wish to continue further south you should take care along the B2135 as far as the next traffic-free section. The final stage into Bramber via King's Stone Avenue and Castle Lane is on narrow, if minor, roads with no cycle lanes and sometimes no pavement. A mixture of railway path, stone-based track and minor lanes is used south to Bramber with its fine castle and pub.

On your bikes!

1. Start by the silver bike sculptures, by the war memorial, opposite Lintot Square and the Lintot pub in Southwater.

2. Go past Southwater Country Park and cross a minor road. Leave tarmac by a red-brick pumping station, bearing right to join the railway paths.

3. Views of the South Downs open up. About 5 miles after leaving Southwater you will come across a sign for the Partridge Inn in Partridge Green. You may wish to turn around here.

4. To continue south on the Downs Link, join the B2135 (take care, it is sometimes busy), turn right, ignore the first left to Star Trading Estate and take the next left, signposted 'Downs Link'. Tarmac turns to track. At a crossroads turn right to rejoin the railway paths.

5. After almost 2 miles, at the end of the railway path, turn left then right downhill opposite the Old Railway pub. As the road swings left at the bottom, turn right (Holland Lane) then shortly left to rejoin the railway path. There is one short section across a field.

6. After 2 miles, cross the river and follow the track as it swings right uphill. At the T-junction at the top turn left downhill and keep following 'Downs Link' signs on to tarmac and into Bramber, turning left on to King's Stone Avenue and left again on to Castle Lane (keep a close eye out for signs); **take care** as these are narrow roads with poor bike and pedestrian provision and limited visibility.

Refreshments: Lots of choice in Southwater: lakeside cafe at Southwater Country Park. Partridge Inn at Partridge Green. The Old Railway pub, Henfield. Castle Inn Hotel and Old Tollgate Hotel in Bramber.

Bike hire and repairs: Mountain bike hire available from Southwater Watersports (in Southwater Country Park). Repairs from The Bike Side, Partridge Green (cafe on-site).

Public transport and bike links: Christ's Hospital station, 2.5 miles from start; Downs Link provides almost entirely traffic-free route. From Bramber, Downs Link can be followed to Old Shoreham (see next ride). Shoreham-by-Sea station 4.5 miles from Bramber. The Downs Link continues north and south.

Parking: Short-stay free car park, Lintot Square. Paid car park at Southwater Country Park. Free car park in Bramber village.

Maps and guides: OS Landranger 198, Explorer OL11 & OL34.

Website: *www.westsussex.gov.uk/leisure-recreation-and-community/walking-horse-riding-and-cycling/downs-link*

Start
Silver bike sculptures, opposite Lintot Square (51.0241, -0.3516, TQ 157262) or Southwater Country Park (51.0206, -0.3452, TQ 162259)

Finish
Castle Lane, Bramber (50.8823, -0.3167, TQ 185105)

Distance
12 miles/19km.

Category
Railway paths.

Other facilities

27

Ride 7 Downs Link: Bramber to Old Shoreham

Start
The Street, Bramber, near roundabout with A283 (50.8819, -0.3164, TQ 185105)

Finish
The Bridge pub, Old Shoreham (50.8323, -0.2785, TQ 213050)

Distance
4.5 miles/7km.

Category
Railway paths.

Other facilities

NB There is one difficult road crossing near the start of the ride. Please take **EXTREME CARE** crossing the A283 just south of Bramber. Alternatively start from the church in Old Shoreham and ride north as far as the A283.

The most southerly section of the Downs Link, this part of the trail crosses the South Downs Way and continues south to Old Shoreham. Bramber is an attractive village at the edge of the South Downs, located on the banks of the tidal River Adur, one of only three rivers that flows south from the Weald, cutting a course through the chalk hills of the South Downs. This ride runs south from Bramber alongside the river to Old Shoreham, where there is a choice of refreshment stops. There is plenty of wildlife to see along the river, and fine views of Lancing College from the southern end of the ride.

On your bikes!

1. There is a 'Downs Link' sign immediately **before** the roundabout with the A283 in Bramber, directing you on to a track running parallel with the southbound A283. Follow for $1/2$ mile.

2. TAKE EXTREME CARE crossing the A283 to the other side. Wait patiently until there is a clear gap in the traffic for you to cross. After $3/4$ mile at the T-junction of tracks turn left, signposted 'South Downs Way, Eastbourne'. Cross the river bridge then turn right, signposted 'Coastal Link'.

Refreshments: Castle Inn Hotel and Old Tollgate pub in Bramber. Lots of choice in Old Shoreham.
Bike hire and repairs: Several bike shops in Shoreham-by-Sea.
Public transport and bike links: Shoreham-by-Sea station, $1/2$ mile from end. Downs Link extends north to Guildford.
Parking: Free car park in Bramber village. Paid car park in Shoreham town centre.
Maps and guides: OS Landranger 198, Explorer OL11.
Website: www.westsussex.gov.uk/leisure-recreation-and-community/walking-horse-riding-and-cycling/downs-link

3. Follow the track alongside the river for 3 miles, passing under a large road bridge, ignoring a wooden bridge to the right, passing under a railway bridge and alongside the riverside apartments. The surface varies in quality.

4. The path ends at the Bridge pub on the roundabout at the junction of the A283/A259 in Old Shoreham. Retrace your steps.

SOUTHERN COUNTIES

Brighton Promenade Ride 8

Ever more seaside resorts in the south of England are creating cycle paths along the wide promenades that run parallel with the coast, offering cyclists the chance to glide along from one end of a resort to the other with fine views out to sea, and myriad opportunities to stop for refreshments. This route through Brighton passes the famous Brighton Pier and continues on to Rottingdean, where you've the option of a high-level route along the clifftop or a route at sea level beneath the towering chalk cliffs. Why not go out on one option and return on the other? There is another traffic-free section of promenade between Worthing and Shoreham-by-Sea.

On your bikes!
East from Hove Lagoon towards Rottingdean

1. The route is well waymarked as National Cycle Network (NCN) Route 2. Signs on the ground, painted cycle lanes and 'No Cycling' signs will all give you a clear indication of the course of the route, at times right by the seafront, at other times set back from it.

2. Go past Brighton Pier and towards the marina. The route climbs up away from the seafront. At the top of the climb you have a choice: **(a)** bear left through the subway under the A259 to join the clifftop path past the windmill to Rottingdean, to finish at the White Horse Hotel, or **(b)** bear right downhill to join the Undercliff Walk, running beneath the towering chalk cliffs on a wide concrete path that also leads to Rottingdean.

Refreshments: Lots of choice all along the seafront and in Rottingdean.
Bike hire and repairs: BTN BikeShare scheme; docking stations on seafront (for example, Peace Statue and pier). Bike hire from Brighton Beach Bikes at pier. Several bike shops in Brighton.
Public transport and bike links: Several stations between Portslade and Brighton rail stations, within 1 mile of the promenade. Route is part of NCN 2, linking Kent to Cornwall.
Parking: Parking in central Brighton can be very expensive; route is well-served by public transport. Paid car parks at Shoreham docks and Rottingdean.
Maps and guides: OS Landranger 198, Explorer OL11.
Website: *www.sustrans.org.uk/find-a-route-on-the-national-cycle-network/south-coast-promenades-worthing-to-brighton*

Start
Between Hove Lagoon (50.8267, -0.2009, TQ 268046) and Brighton Marina, Brighton (50.8119, -0.0921, TQ 345031)

Finish
White Horse Hotel, Rottingdean (50.8026, -0.0577, TQ 370021)

Distance
7 miles/11km.

Category
Seafront promenade.

Other facilities

NB *Please ride responsibly along the promenade, especially during busy summer weekends; pay attention to the cycling signs and be aware that the paths are shared with pedestrians.*

29

Ride 9 Ditchling Beacon on the South Downs Way

Start
Junction of School Lane and A273, Pyecombe
(50.8996, -0.1618, TQ 294127)

Finish
HMP Lewes, Lewes
(50.8738, -0.0064, TQ 404101)

Distance
8.5 miles/14km.

Category
Grassy tracks, chalk-topped trails.

Other facilities

The 100-mile South Downs Way, which connects Winchester to Eastbourne, is one of only two National Trails that can be cycled in its entirety (the other being the Pennine Bridleway). The trail is sometimes on quiet country lanes but most usually on grassy trods or chalky tracks; it can be muddy and slippery, and is best tackled on sunny summer days. This section climbs over Ditchling Beacon, the highest point in East Sussex. With a cumulative ascent of 170 metres, often on grassy tracks, this is an energetic ride best tackled by confident riders on gravel or mountain bikes. Your reward for hard efforts will be panoramic views over the South Downs and the sea.

On your bikes!

1. Join the South Downs Way, just north of Pyecombe, where School Lane meets the main A273 road; there is a track that runs next to the road. After 150m, turn right through Pyecombe Golf Club; **take care** when crossing the A273 here.

2. Follow the way for 3/4 mile past the clubhouse and through the golf course – watch out for golfballs! At a crossroads of tracks, turn left heading towards the Jack and Jill windmills. Turn right, in front of the windmills. Continue straight on to climb the ridge to the summit of Ditchling Beacon, ignoring the other paths and tracks that criss-cross the South Downs Way.

3. Around 250m after the summit of Ditchling Beacon, you reach the car park; there is almost always an ice cream van here in the summer. **Take care** passing through the car park and the road as this is popular with drivers and road cyclists; the Tour de France climbed Ditchling Beacon in 1994. You can turn right on to

Refreshments: The Plough pub and Wild Bean Cafe in Pyecombe. Lots of choice in Lewes. Often ice cream van in Ditchling Beacon car park.
Bike hire and repairs: Hassocks Community Cycle Hire. Sussex Bike Hire in Lewes. More options in Brighton. Spares and repairs from Lewes Cycleshack.
Public transport and bike links: Hassocks station, 1.5 miles from windmills via bridleway and road, but no way to avoid A723 UNLESS you walk/ push your bikes along footpath next to railway (1 mile, cycling forbidden). Lewes station, 3/4 mile from end.
Parking: Limited on-street parking in Pyecombe. Car park on Mill Lane, next to Jack and Jill windmills. On-street parking (paid) near end; paid car parks in Lewes centre.
Maps and guides: OS Landranger 198, Explorer OL11.
Website: www.nationaltrail.co.uk/en_GB/trails/south-downs-way

Ditchling Road here; it is an easy, downhill 2.5-mile ride to the outskirts of Brighton.

4. If you want to continue on from Ditchling Beacon, cross Ditchling Road and continue on the South Downs Way, ignoring tracks to the left and right; there are some climbs to tackle. After 2.5 miles, the South Downs Way turns right – do not follow it, but remain straight ahead on the bridleway that skirts below the peak of Blackcap. Continue to follow the bridleway as it descends, bending towards the right; ignore other tracks to the left.

5. Continue straight ahead past the old racecourse and Blackcap Bikes to pass HMP Lewes and reach the outskirts of the town centre.

SOUTHERN COUNTIES

Egrets Way: Monk's House to Newhaven
Ride 10

The Egrets Way is a new recreational cycle route that aims to link Lewes to Newhaven, following the River Ouse, and aims to create a link from the South Downs Way to Lewes. The route is often unsurfaced, and this is a great trail for gravel bikes. The route between Monk's House and Peacehaven, which is now open, is described below, but there are other sections to explore (for example, between Lewes and Swanborough) and new sections are being added, so it is well worth checking the website. The ride starts near Monk's House, the sixteenth-century National Trust cottage which was once the beloved country getaway of Virginia and Leonard Woolf.

On your bikes!

1. The bridleway begins 100m past Monk's House: it begins to the left of a car park entrance. Follow the bridleway on reasonable farm tracks for nearly 1 mile to the banks of the River Ouse.

2. The trail joins the Egrets Way by the River Ouse; turn right on to a rougher riverside trail. Follow the Way for 1 mile.

3. The Egrets Way crosses the South Downs Way near Southease; it is possible to turn right on to the South Downs Way to complete a circular route back to Monk's House. If you want to continue to follow the Egrets Way, continue straight ahead, still by the river.

4. After a little more than 1 mile, the Egrets Way reaches a road. Turn left on to the road for 150m; there is a pavement along this section if you would prefer to avoid the traffic. Cross the road – **take care** – to a bridleway on the right. Continue on the bridleway for 3/4 mile, ignoring tracks to the left and right.

5. Shortly after Halcombe Farm, fork left. At a track junction, turn right to reach the outskirts of Peacehaven.

Refreshments: Abergavenny Arms, Rodmell; cafe at YHA South Downs, Southease. Lots of choice in Peacehaven.
Bike hire and repairs: Sussex Bike Hire in Seahaven. Cycle shops in Lewes and Brighton.
Public transport and bike links: Newhaven Town station, 3.5 miles from end; Southease station, 1/2 mile from route. The route crosses the South Downs Way bridleway. National Cycle Network (NCN) Route 2 runs through Peacehaven.
Parking: Limited on-street parking in Rodmell. On-street car parking in Peacehaven; paid car parks near seafront.
Maps and guides: OS Landranger 198, Explorer OL11.
Website: www.egretsway.org.uk

Start
Monk's House, Rodmell (50.8396, 0.0167, TQ 421064)

Finish
Telscombe Road, Peacehaven (50.8060, 0.0087, TQ 416026)

Distance
4.5 miles/7km.

Category
Riverside paths, farm tracks.

Other facilities

Ride 11 Friston Forest

Start
Seven Sisters Country Park Visitor Centre, Exceat (50.7752, 0.1535, TV 519995)

Finish
Cuckmere Haven (sea route) (50.7604, 0.1494, TV 517978) or same as start (forest route)

Distance
5 miles/8km (forest route); 2.5 miles/4km (sea route).

Category
Forest trails, stone tracks.

Other facilities

There are two rides starting from Exceat, where the River Cuckmere has cut a course through the chalk ridge of the South Downs. This short ride goes to the coast and back; the longer ride is a waymarked forest route. The visitor centre for the Seven Sisters Country Park is housed in a converted eighteenth-century barn at Exceat Farm. For those seeking a more adrenaline-fuelled forest adventure, there is also the 5.5-mile red grade (for experienced riders) Jeremy Cole mountain bike trail around the forest.

On your bikes!
Route to the sea

1. Push your bike past the cafe and visitor centre. Cross the busy A259 by the bus stop, signposted 'To the beach, Foxholes'. **TAKE GREAT CARE**.

2. Follow the track through Seven Sisters Country Park for $3/4$ mile then as the concrete track swings left towards Foxholes, bear right on to a gravel track for fine sea views. Retrace your steps.

Waymarked forest route

1. From the car park by the visitor centre, go back towards the exit then turn right at a square wooden post, signposted 'Bridleway to West Dean'. Join the family cycle trail at a green and white 'Friston Forest' sign.

2. At the track junction with the brick and flint Pond Cottage ahead, bear right to join a better gravel track. Follow this long,

wide, straight forest road, passing flint houses on the left and going round a metal barrier across the road. At the crossroads of wide tracks by tall red and white poles, go straight ahead.

3. After almost $1/2$ mile the path narrows then swings left and starts climbing. Shortly turn left uphill off the wide gravel track on to a stone and earth track, soon turning left again (all signposted).

4. Long, gentle descent on an earth and grass track. At a crossroads with a smooth forest road turn right gently uphill. After $1/4$ mile turn left on a similar broad forest road. Climb to the highpoint with the option of turning right up to the viewpoint (rough and steep). For the main route continue straight ahead downhill.

5. At the T-junction with a forest road at the bottom of a fun, grassy descent, turn right to rejoin the outward route back to the start.

Refreshments: Cafe at start. Pubs nearby in Litlington, Seaford and Alfriston.
Bike hire and repairs: Hires, spares and repairs from Cuckmere Cycle Co, Exceat or Let's Bike – Eastbourne. Spares and repairs from Mr Cycles, Seaford.
Public transport and bike links:
Seaford station, 2.5 miles from start. National Cycle Network (NCN) Route 2, linking Kent to Cornwall, passes Friston Forest; it links with the South Downs Way long-distance bridleway in Alfriston.
Parking: Litlington Road or Exceat Forestry England (paid) car parks.
Maps and guides: OS Landranger 199, Explorer OL25.
Website: *www.forestryengland.uk/friston-forest*

SOUTHERN COUNTIES

Cuckoo Trail   Ride 12

The Cuckoo Trail is one of the longest and most popular railway paths in the South East. The line gained its name because of a Sussex tradition that the first cuckoo of spring was released each year at Heathfield Cuckoo Fair. It offers superb traffic-free cycling through a mixture of broadleaf woodland, open grassland, arable farmland and pasture. As you head down towards Polegate there are views of the rolling chalk hills of the South Downs ahead of you. Along the way are metal sculptures, an arch in the form of a Chinese pagoda roof and plenty of carved wooden seats with a variety of motifs, made from local oaks blown down in the great storm of 1987. The verges are thick with wildflowers. There is a gentle climb up from Polegate to Heathfield so that you can look forward to a gravity-assisted return journey! In several places along the way, bridges have been dismantled and houses built on the course of the railway, requiring you to cross several minor roads and use short sections of estate roads through Hailsham and Horam to regain the railway path. The route description begins from Polegate, although the Cuckoo Trail begins three miles further south at Hampden Park.

On your bikes!

1. From Polegate, follow the railway path for 3 miles into Hailsham. At this point the route follows estate roads so look out for 'Cuckoo Trail (bikes)' signs.

2. Rejoin the railway path and follow for 5 miles through to Horam. There is a second, short section on estate roads.

3. The trail ends after a further 3 miles in Heathfield. In this final section there are several roads to cross – mainly quiet lanes, but care should still be taken if you are with young children.

Refreshments: Lots of choice in each of the towns. Cuckoo Shack Cafe on trail, just north of Polegate.
Bike hire and repairs: Countrybike hire (via app) available en route. Bicycle shops in Heathfield, Horam, Hailsham and Polegate.
Public transport and bike links: Polegate station, 1/2 mile from Cuckoo Trail start. National Cycle Network (NCN) Route 21 continues to London (on- and off-road).
Parking: On-street parking in Polegate; paid car park at Polegate rail station. Free trail car parks at Heathfield, Horam, Hellingly and Hailsham.
Maps and guides: OS Landranger 199, Explorer OL25; maps of the trail and circular routes available from website below.
Website: www.eastsussex.gov.uk/leisureandtourism/discover-east-sussex/countryside-sites/cuckootrail

Start
School Lane, Polegate
(50.8244, 0.2470, TQ 584052)

Finish
Junction of Newnham Way and Station Road, Heathfield
(50.9685, 0.2515, TQ 582212)

Distance
11 miles/18km.

Category
Railway paths.

Other facilities

33

Ride 13   Deers Leap Park

Start/finish
Deers Leap Park reception, East Grinstead (51.1051, -0.0247, TQ 384358)

Distance
3 miles/5km.

Category
Hard-surfaced trails, optional technical tracks.

Other facilities

Deers Leap is a privately owned, 230-acre park, which was bought in the 1990s by the Hobbs family, who wanted to create an outdoor activity space. There is a (reasonable) admission fee to cover the cost of trail maintenance and creation. There is a family friendly trail around the park, that is well-signposted and has no technical track. There are also more technical trails through a woodland area and a skills area. The park also offers a cafe, an outdoor adventure area and bike hire.

On your bikes!

1. Follow the surfaced track from the park entrance. By the duck pond, you can fork left to take a shortcut on an unsurfaced track or remain on the hard-surfaced track. Whichever way you choose, turn left at the next track junction.

2. Follow the track to the bottom of the park and follow it as it turns right up the edge of the park.

3. When you reach marker post 14, you should turn right if you wish to remain on surfaced track, or you can continue straight on, bending right later. Both options return to the start.

Refreshments: Cafe at the start.
Bike hire and repairs: Hire, spares and repairs from the Bike Shop in Deers Leap Park.
Public transport and bike links: East Grinstead station, 2 miles from Deers Leap Park.
Parking: Parking at start (included in park admission).
Maps and guides: Available from website.
Website: deersleap.co.uk

Worth Way west of East Grinstead — Ride 14

One of two railway paths that start in East Grinstead, the Worth Way whisks you away from commuter land into a wooded landscape in the twinkling of an eye. There is a $1/2$-mile section along roads through Crawley Down before you dive back into woodland once again. The route ends at Worth (on the eastern edge of Crawley). As with the Forest Way (next ride), this forms part of National Cycle Network (NCN) Route 21, the Downs & Weald Cycle Route between London and the south coast.

On your bikes!

1. From the signpost in the corner of the station car park, follow the Worth Way for 2.5 miles, at which point the track turns to tarmac. Three T-junctions! At the first, at the end of Cob Close, turn left; at the second, at the end of Hazel Way, turn right; at the third, at the end of Woodland Drive, turn left.

2. At the offset crossroads at the end of Burleigh Way, go straight ahead on to Old Station Close. The tarmac turns to track. Continue in the same direction at the next crossroads.

3. At the next road, by a brick and slate building, turn left then shortly right through Rowfant car park.

4. The railway path ends at the third road (by Keepers Cottage) but it is possible to continue a further mile to the church at Worth on a good, stone-based bridleway. Cross the road and turn left on to the track along the verge. On a sharp left-hand bend after 200m, turn right and follow this track in the same direction for 1 mile, past a farm and over the M23 as far as Worth, perhaps visiting its lovely Anglo-Saxon church.

Refreshments: Lots of choice in East Grinstead.
Bike hire and repairs: Spares and repairs from Halfords, East Grinstead and On Your Bike on Felbridge Forge.
Public transport and bike links: Trail starts at East Grinstead station. Three Bridges station, 1.5 miles from Worth, largely off-road on continuation of Worth Way.
Parking: Paid car park at East Grinstead station. Limited on-street parking near end.
Maps and guides: OS Landranger 187, Explorer 135.
Website: www.westsussex.gov.uk/leisure-recreation-and-community/walking-horse-riding-and-cycling/worth-way

Start
East Grinstead rail station, East Grinstead (51.1270, -0.0184, TQ 388383)

Finish
Worth, near Crawley (51.1108, -0.1426, TQ 301363)

Distance
6.5 miles/10.5km.

Category
Railway paths.

Other facilities

Ride 15 Forest Way east of East Grinstead

Start
Chequer Mead Theatre, East Grinstead (51.1259, -0.0043, TQ 397381)

Finish
Corseley Road, Groombridge (51.1079, 0.1822, TQ 529365)

Distance
11 miles/18km.

Category
Railway paths.

Other facilities

The countryside around Hartfield is the setting of A.A. Milne's Winnie-the-Pooh stories, so watch out for Tiggers and Heffalumps! This fine ride passes through woodland and arable land lying between East Grinstead and Groombridge. There are picnic tables along the way and the broad, good-quality track makes an ideal ride for exercise and conversation. The railway path forms part of National Cycle Network (NCN) Route 21, the Downs & Weald Cycle Route between London and the south coast. The railway line was opened by the London, Brighton & South Coast Railway in 1866 as an extension of the Three Bridges to East Grinstead branch line. Forest Row was the busiest of the intermediate stations, dealing in minerals and general goods. It was finally closed as part of the Beeching cuts in 1966.

On your bikes!

1. From the car park, return to De La Warr Road and turn right. At the T-junction with College Lane, turn right for 100m then turn first left downhill by a stone wall. At the end of Old Road, cross to the opposite pavement, turn left then right through the fence on to the path. At the next road go straight ahead on to Forest Way.

2. After 2 miles, use the toucan crossing to cross the busy A22 and continue straight ahead on to a tarmac drive, signposted 'Tablehurst Farm'. After 350m, shortly after passing Forest Row Pumping Station on your left, near the end of a line of cypress trees, turn right on to a narrow path, signposted 'Forest Way Country Park'.

3. After 4 miles, at a T-junction, just after going through a large, yellow, stone bridge under the B2026, turn left then right past Hartfield station, which is now a private house.

4. The Forest Way continues for a further 3.5 miles to the edge of Groombridge, crossing several minor roads. To visit the pub, shop or bakery turn left at the T-junction with the lane (by a pumping station) and follow up and down for $1/2$ mile into the village.

Refreshments: Lots of choice in East Grinstead. Good pubs just off the route in Hartfield, Withyham and Groombridge.
Bike hire and repairs: Hire from Countrybike at Groombridge station (via app). Spares and repairs from Halfords, East Grinstead.
Public transport and bike links: East Grinstead station, 1 mile from start. Groombridge station, on the heritage Spa Valley Railway (bikes allowed); it connects with national rail services at Eridge and Tunbridge Wells. NCN 18 and 21 meet at Groombridge.
Parking: Paid Chequer Mead car park on De La Warr Road, East Grinstead. Free car park in Groombridge on Station Road (next to village hall).
Maps and guides: OS Landranger 187 & 188, Explorer 135.
Website: www.sustrans.org.uk/find-a-route-on-the-national-cycle-network/forest-way

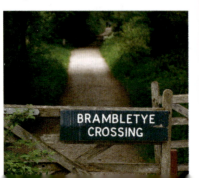

SOUTHERN COUNTIES

Tudor Trail: Ride 16
Tonbridge to Penshurst Place

The Tudor Trail between Tonbridge Castle and Penshurst Place offers an excellent, almost entirely traffic-free ride from the heart of Tonbridge alongside the River Medway, out into the countryside as far as the glorious buildings of Penshurst Place, some five miles to the west. The ride takes you past playing fields on the edge of Tonbridge and into Haysden Country Park, running around the edge of Barden Lake with its wide variety of birdlife. Shortly after passing beneath the A21 you enter a delightful secret kingdom of lush broadleaf woodland, carpeted with wildflowers in the spring and a delight in autumn as the colours change. The one noticeable climb of the day comes between the bridge over the River Medway and Well Place Day Nursery, giving you wide-ranging views of the surrounding countryside and setting you up for a fine descent past two lakes to arrive at Penshurst Place, the finest and most complete example in England of fourteenth-century domestic architecture.

On your bikes!

1. From the entrance to Tonbridge Swimming Pool car park, by a 'Children' road sign, take the cycle path signposted to Penshurst. Follow National Cycle Network (NCN) Route 12 signs into woodland and over a series of bridges with metal railings.

2. Emerge at Barden Lake, turn left and keep the water to your right. At the end of the lake turn left to go under a railway bridge, then at the T-junction, with the car park to the right, turn left. At the next T-junction, at the end of the approach road to Haysden Country Park, turn right, signposted 'Penshurst Bike Route'.

Refreshments: Lots of choice in Tonbridge. Cafe at Penshurst Place (outside entrance).
Bike hire and repairs: Countrybike hire at Penshurst Place; several bike shops in Tonbridge, including Cycle-Ops, next to the castle, 250m from start.
Public transport and bike links: Tonbridge station, 1/2 mile from start. Leigh station, 2 miles from end; easiest way to get there is to retrace your tracks to road crossed in step 4, turn left on road for 1/2 mile.
Parking: Paid car park next to Tonbridge Swimming Pool. Free car park at Penshurst Place.
Maps and guides: OS Landranger 188, Explorer 147.
Website: www.sustrans.org.uk/find-a-route-on-the-national-cycle-network/tudor-trail

3. Follow this lane through the village of Lower Haysden, past the pub, under the A21, turn first right then left on to a stone track, signposted 'Public Bridleway'. Follow the excellently sign-posted track through lovely broadleaf woodland.

4. At the end of the track, at the T-junction with a road, turn right then shortly after crossing the bridge take the first concrete track to the left, signposted 'Penshurst 1.5 miles'.

5. Climb on this broad concrete track then descend past Well Place Day Nursery towards the magnificent buildings of Penshurst Place.

Start
Tonbridge Swimming Pool, near the castle, Tonbridge (51.1976, 0.2714, TQ 588467)

Finish
Penshurst Place, Tonbridge (51.1731, 0.1843, TQ 528438)

Distance
5.5 miles/9km.

Category
Stone-based cycle paths.

Other facilities

Ride 17 Bewl Water Lamberhurst

Start/finish
Bewl Water's Waterfront Cafe, Kent (51.0790, 0.3907, TQ 676337)

Distance
13 miles/21km.

Category
Round reservoir.

Other facilities

NB This is a very popular route with walkers and horse riders – please give way to them and ride with consideration for others at all times.

A round-reservoir route south of London, Bewl Water offers a fine, challenging summer ride through woodland and pasture on a mixture of tracks and quiet lanes. Be warned that there are some steep hills on the lane sections and that on some of the off-road stretches the surface can be rough. The route should be avoided after prolonged rain. It is shut from November to the end of April. As a full 13-mile circuit, it is not suitable for young children. The dam is made from local clay and faced with concrete slabs to prevent erosion. Holding back 6,900 million gallons of water, Bewl Water is the largest stretch of open water in the South East. Nearby Chingley Wood is a mixed coppice woodland once used for fuelling ironworks in the valley. Several willow plantations around the lake produce timber for the manufacture of cricket bats.

On your bikes!

1. From the cafe, head down towards the dam and follow bike signs. The route is waymarked with 'Round Water Route' signs but the waymarking is patchy and it is not sufficient to say 'follow the edge of the lake' as the route veers away from the water's edge on the southern part of the ride. A map is useful for the first time you ride the circuit. On the tarmac sections, keep an eye out for 'Round Water Route' signs at each junction.

Refreshments: At visitor centre or the Bull Inn at Three Leg Cross, about halfway around the circuit.
Bike hire and repairs: Bike hire at Bewl Water, next to cafe.
Public transport and bike links: Wadhurst station, 3 miles from Bewl Water.
Parking: Paid parking at start.
Maps and guides: OS Landranger 188, Explorer 136.
Website: *www.bewlwater.co.uk*

SOUTHERN COUNTIES

Bedgebury Forest Ride 18

Bedgebury Forest is a Forestry England holding in Kent with waymarked bike routes. There is a 5.5-mile circuit aimed at families and an 8-mile, tougher (red grade) singletrack course for more experienced mountain bikers. Bedgebury is mixed woodland, and in amongst the fir and conifers you will find sweet chestnut, birch, oak and sycamore, not to mention bright yellow ragwort, purple willowherb and foxgloves. The forest lies adjacent to Bedgebury Pinetum, which contains a magnificent collection of rare trees and flowering shrubs. There is a lovely picnic spot by the lakes that you pass along the route.

On your bikes!

1. The blue family trail begins near the visitor centre and takes a well-waymarked loop around the south of the forest on wide, stone-topped forestry tracks. It can be ridden as a shorter beginner-friendly, 3-mile trail by taking a shortcut across the centre of the forest – the longer route extends to the forest's eastern edges. The loop can be ridden in either direction. There are some gentle inclines and declines. Some sections of the route coincide with walkers' trails, and you may encounter walkers and horse riders on any section of the route. **Watch out** for mountain bikers on the red trail at junctions.

2. The red-grade mountain bike trail starts south of the visitor centre, near the Flimwell radio mast; the start can be reached by following the blue trail anticlockwise from the visitor centre. The trail, which follows a wiggly route around the whole forest, must be ridden in a clockwise direction. The trail offers plenty of challenging climbs and descents, drop-offs, berms and rocks. The trail finishes near the visitor centre.

Refreshments: Cafe at the visitor centre.
Bike hire and repairs: Spares, repairs and hire from Quench Cycles, near Go Ape in Bedgebury Forest.
Public transport and bike links: Etchingham rail station, 5 miles south of forest. National Cycle Network (NCN) Route 18, which links Canterbury to Royal Tunbridge Wells, passes through Bedgebury Forest.
Parking: Paid parking at start.
Maps and guides: OS Landranger 188, Explorer 136.
Website: *www.forestryengland.uk/bedgebury*

Start/finish
Bedgebury Forest visitor centre, near Flimwell (51.0728, 0.4487, TQ 716332)

Distance
5.5 miles/9km (blue forest track) or 8 miles/13km (red mountain bike trail).

Category
Forest trails or mountain bike tracks.

Other facilities

39

Ride 19 Rye Harbour Nature Reserve Loop

Start
Winchelsea Beach Cafe, Rye Harbour Nature Reserve (50.9087, 0.7188, TQ 912157)

Finish
Rye Harbour Discovery Centre, Rye Harbour (50.9342, 0.7675, TQ 946186)

Distance
3.5 miles/5.5km.

Category
Tarmac shared-use paths.

Other facilities

The Rye Harbour Nature Reserve is a popular birdwatching destination. There is a shared-use trail next to Rye's sand and shingle beaches. Wildlife aside, this is a trail with plenty of history to divert you: the Napoleonic Martello tower, the World War II bunkers and the Mary Stanford Lifeboat House that stands in tribute to a 1928 tragedy when all 17 of the lifeboat crew drowned. The trail starts at a cafe and ends at the Rye Harbour Discovery Centre. There are narrow gates to negotiate on the route and a short section on access roads.

On your bikes!

1. The trail begins 200m south-west of the cafe; turn left to follow it along the edge of the beach.

2. After 3 miles, turn left. The traffic-free section ends 700m further on by the Rye Harbour Discovery Centre. The trail can be followed a further 3.5 miles on to Rye; there are short sections on-road but the route is largely traffic free.

Refreshments: Cafe at start and finish; lots of choice in Rye.
Bike hire and repairs: Hire from Harbour Cycles, near Rye Harbour Discovery Centre.
Public transport and bike links: Winchelsea station, 3 miles from start, via National Cycle Network (NCN) Route 2 (on-road). Rye station, 3.5 miles from end, via Harbour Trail (largely off-road).
Parking: Free parking at start.
Maps and guides: OS Landranger 189, Explorer 125.
Website: *sussexwildlifetrust.org.uk/visit/rye-harbour/about-rye-harbour-nature-reserve*

SOUTHERN COUNTIES

The Medway Towpath Ride 20

The Medway Towpath was created in 2017; it provides a traffic-free cycle route from Aylesford to Barming, via Maidstone, for walkers and cyclists. There are short (well-marked) sections, where cyclists must dismount. The trail is well-surfaced and suitable for any bike and rider, and there are plenty of opportunities to stop for tea and cake. If you're lucky, you may glimpse a kingfisher.

On your bikes!

1. The trail can be joined at the corner of the car park next to Aylesford Bridge. Follow the towpath along the banks of the River Medway past an industrial estate and under the M20 motorway.

2. The route turns away from the river, on shared-use tracks by roads, to divert briefly through Maidstone, passing Maidstone East station.

3. The route returns to the riverbank near the Fremlin Walk shopping centre. The trail follows the river towpath until Barming Bridge; there is a short, well-signed section by East Farleigh where cyclists must dismount because the towpath is narrow.

Refreshments: Plenty of choice on and close to route at Aylesford, Allington Lock, Maidstone and East Farleigh.
Bike hire and repairs: Spares and repairs from Evans Cycles, Halfords and Cycles UK in Maidstone.
Public transport and bike links: Aylesford station, 3/4 mile from start. East Farleigh station, 1 mile from end (via towpath). Maidstone East station also en route.
Parking: Free Station Road car park at start.
Maps and guides: OS Landranger 188, Explorer 148.
Website: *explorekent.org/activities/river-medway-towpath-cycle-route*

Start
Aylesford Bridge, Aylesford (51.3027, 0.4821, TQ 730589)

Finish
Barming Bridge, East Barming (51.2584, 0.4695, TQ 724539)

Distance
6.5 miles/10.5km.

Category
Canal towpaths.

Other facilities

© DAVE PARNELL

41

Ride 21 North Downs Way: Lenham to Charing

Start
Faversham Road, Lenham (51.2437, 0.7226, TQ 901529)

Finish
A252, Charing (51.2150, 0.8000, TQ 957499)

Distance
8.5 miles/13km.

Category
Restricted byways, bridleways, sometimes singletrack.

Other facilities

Unlike its southern counterpart, the North Downs Way cannot be cycled in its entirety, although Cycling UK have created a Rider's Route alternative. Much of the North Downs Way does, however, follow bridleways: the section between Lenham and Charing is described here. This section is also part of the Pilgrims Cycle Trail between Rochester and Canterbury. There are very short sections on the road. The trail is generally tarmac or gravel topped and might be tackled on a road bike in good conditions with care, but it would be much more enjoyable on a gravel or hybrid bike.

On your bikes!
1. The trail begins on Faversham Road; turn right on to the restricted byway in front of Kent Cottage. Follow the tarmac lane past houses; the lane soon gives way to gravel track, which offers a fine view of the Lenham Cross.

2. When you reach the road, turn left to follow Hubbards Hill for 400m. As the road bends sharply left, stay straight on a stony track. Follow to Rayners Hill road, where you turn left and almost immediately right to remain on byway. The track becomes narrower as it crosses farm fields and through hedgerow, but remains hard surfaced.

3. At Hart Hill road, turn right, and then left back on to a track after 60m. The route emerges on road on the outskirts of Charing. Turn right in front of Twyford House, follow the lane to the A252 main road. **Cross with care** and continue straight on if you wish to visit the village centre.

Refreshments: The Dog and Bear Hotel, Lenham. Purple Patch bakery, Charing; Charing Tearooms at Bookmakers Arms pub, Charing.
Public transport and bike links: Lenham station, 1 mile from start. Charing station, 1/2 mile from end.
Parking: Free on-street parking in Lenham and Charing.
Maps and guides: OS Landranger 189, Explorer 137 & 149.
Website: www.nationaltrail.co.uk/en_GB/trails/north-downs-way

SOUTHERN COUNTIES

Hythe Seafront Ride 22

This is surely one of the finest seafront cycle routes on the English south coast. Other cycling promenades such as Bournemouth or Brighton may be full of things to see, but they are also very popular with pedestrians and much of your time is spent looking out for other people. Here, for much of the time you can enjoy the views out over the English Channel without fear of the crowds. There are two very contrasting ways of extending this ride: continuing east along National Cycle Network (NCN) Route 2 you will be faced with a climb of around 180 metres up on to the famous white cliffs between Folkestone and Dover; to the west the Royal Military Canal leads to the amazing network of quiet, flat lanes that criss-cross Romney Marsh, an area as flat as the Somerset Levels or the Fenland of East Anglia.

On your bikes!

1. From Hythe rail station, turn left and use the pedestrian crossing to cross the road; take the riverside path straight ahead that follows the Royal Military Canal. After 300m, reach Dymchurch Road; use the crossing to cross the road, turn left across the bridge and right on to the canal towpath.

2. At the end of Portland Road, cross Stade Street on to a tarmac drive alongside the canal. Shortly, opposite a blue metal bridge on the left, turn right on to Ladies Walk (NCN 2) by the Hythe Bowling Club. Cross the road on to Moyle Tower Road to join the wide, red, tarmac promenade. Turn left.

3. The promenade turns from red tarmac to white concrete. It ends after almost 5 miles just before Folkestone Harbour Arm. You may prefer to turn around at this point and return to Hythe. If you wish to visit Folkestone, bear left away from the sea towards the fringe of woodland and follow 'National Cycle Network Route 2' signs along residential roads into town.

Refreshments: Lots of choice in Hythe and Folkestone.
Bike hire and repairs: Click2cycle (docking) bike hire in Folkestone and Hythe. Several bike shops in Folkestone, including Renhams Cycle Centre, 1/2 mile from end.
Public transport and bike links: Hythe station is on the heritage Romney, Hythe and Dymchurch railway; it does not join the mainline; nearest mainline railway is Sandling, 2.5 miles from start. Folkestone station, 1.5 miles from end.
Parking: Free parking at Hythe station; paid parking at Portland Street. Paid parking near seafront in Folkestone.
Maps and guides: OS Landranger 179, Explorer 138.
Website: www.explorekent.org/activities/sandwich-to-rye-cycle-ride

Start
Hythe station, Hythe (51.0716, 1.0729, TR 154347)

Finish
Folkestone Harbour Arm, Folkestone (51.0776, 1.1890, TR 235358)

Distance
5.5 miles/9km.

Category
Seafront promenades, canal towpaths.

Other facilities

43

Ride 23 The Great Stour Way

Start
Station Road car park, Chartham (51.2557, 1.0192, TR 108551)

Finish
Westgate Gardens, Canterbury (51.2795, 1.0723, TR 144579)

Distance
3 miles/5km.

Category
Multi-use, hard-surfaced trails.

Other facilities

The Great Stour Way is a well-surfaced, multi-use trail running from Chartham to Canterbury along the banks of the Great Stour river. It is also the final section of the 47-mile Pilgrims Cycle Trail that links Rochester to Canterbury on bridleways, cycle tracks and quiet lanes. This is a wildlife-rich route, and there are plenty of interpretation boards to enjoy along the trail as well as great spots for a picnic.

On your bikes!

1. The trail begins in the corner of the village car park on Station Road. The trail is straightforward to follow, as it follows the course of the river.

2. The cycle trail finishes on the outskirts of Canterbury, just after passing under the (low) A2050 bridge; cycling is not permitted through Westgate Gardens.

Refreshments: The Artichoke pub, 300m from start. Lots of choice in Canterbury.
Bike hire and repairs: Hire, spares and repairs from Canterbury Cycle Hire, $1/2$ mile from end. Several bike shops in Canterbury.
Public transport and bike links: Chartham station, 200m from start. Canterbury East, $1/2$ mile from end; Canterbury West, $1/2$ mile. Connects with National Cycle Network (NCN) Route 1 in Canterbury.
Parking: Free car park at start. Paid Toddlers Cove car park, 250m from end; paid car parks on Castle Street, Canterbury, $1/2$ mile from end.
Maps and guides: OS Landranger 179, Explorer 150.
Website: *explorekent.org/activities/great-stour-way*

SOUTHERN COUNTIES

Crab and Winkle Way: Canterbury to Whitstable
Ride 24

This ride starts from the centre of the beautiful, historic city of Canterbury and uses traffic-calmed roads and specially built cycle paths to link town to countryside, following the course of a dismantled railway through broadleaf woodland to the attractive seaside town of Whitstable. The streets around Canterbury Cathedral are best explored on foot. The route climbs steadily out of the city with wonderful views opening up behind you. After passing close to the university the route soon joins a traffic-free section that runs for over four miles, past fruit farms and through woodland to South Street on the edge of Whitstable. Cycle paths and traffic-calmed streets lead right into the heart of this fine coastal town.

On your bikes!

1. From Westgate, at the junction of Pound Lane and St Peter's Street in the centre of Canterbury, use the cycle facility to cross the main road and follow the route waymarked 'Route 1, Whitstable' along Westgate Grove and Whitehall Road.

2. The route runs eastwards, parallel with the A2050, then turns north through a more rural setting and climbs steadily. Look behind you and to your right for fine views of Canterbury and the cathedral.

3. Go past a tall white-water tower. Use the toucan crossing to cross the busy Whitstable Road (A290) on to the shared-use pavement. Opposite Kent College turn right on to a tarmac lane that goes past a car park and turns to track as it continues northwards.

4. Descend to cross a stream then climb again, passing fruit orchards and farms. Follow the obvious track into woodland, turning right at the first crossroads then left at a T-junction of forestry tracks. To your left is a pond which was used to cool the winding gear on the old Canterbury & Whitstable Line.

5. After $^3/_4$ mile bear left away from the wide forestry track, descend to cross the bridge over the new A299 and follow the farm track to the road near Brooklands Farm, South Street.

6. Turn left on the road for 300m then immediately after passing Millstrood Road to the left bear left on to the red tarmac cycle path signposted 'Station, Town Centre Cycle Route'. At the end of the cycle path turn left then right downhill through the residential road with sea views ahead.

7. Follow the waymarked route into the heart of Whitstable. It is well worth visiting the harbour. Follow: All Saints Close, railway station, Stream Walk, Albert Street, town centre and harbour.

Refreshments: Lots of choice in Whitstable and Canterbury.
Bike hire and repairs: Repairs and hire from Kent Cycle Hire in Canterbury and Whitstable. Spares and repairs from Herberts Cycles, $^1/_2$ mile from end.
Public transport and bike links: Canterbury West station, 400m from start. Whitstable station, $^1/_2$ mile from end. Route finishes near start of Oyster Bay Trail to Herne Bay.
Parking: Paid car parks on North Lane, near start. Paid car parks near Whitstable Harbour.
Maps and guides: OS Landranger 179, Explorer 150.
Website: explorekent.org/activities/crab-and-winkle-way-canterbury-to-whitstable

Start
Westgate, Canterbury (51.2814, 1.0756, TR 146581)

Finish
Whitstable town centre (51.3629, 1.0275, TR 108670)

Distance
8 miles/13km.

Category
Purpose-built cycle paths, railway paths.

Other facilities

45

Ride 25 The Oyster Bay Trail: Whitstable to Hampton Pier

Start
Oyster Indoor Bowls Centre, Whitstable (51.3640, 1.0286, TR 109671)

Finish
Hampton Pier, Hampton (51.3720, 1.0989, TR 158682)

Distance
3.5 miles/6km.

Category
Shared-use paths.

Other facilities

The Oyster Bay Trail is a promenade route along Kent's seafront from Whitstable to Reculver. The section between Whitstable and Hampton Pier is described here. The trail does continue on through Herne Bay and on to Reculver, where you can connect with the Viking Coastal Trail (next ride), however, there are short sections on road. If you visit during autumn and winter, make sure you enjoy fresh oysters from Whitstable, Britain's oyster capital. Should you wish to continue, the trail takes you to the seafront Central Parade road through Herne Bay for 1.5 miles. This is a traffic-calmed, 20-mile-per-hour road, but the generous provision of parking spaces in preference to safe cycling infrastructure means that you might choose a stroll along the Esplanade rather than an unpleasant ride through an elongated car park.

On your bikes!

1. Join the shared-use, beach-top path by the Oyster Indoor Bowls Centre near the East Quay. Follow the well-surfaced tarmac track – which may be busy, particularly in summer – along the coast.

Refreshments: Plenty of choice en route, and near the start at East Quay.
Bike hire and repairs: Repairs and hire from Kent Cycle Hire in Herne Bay and Whitstable. Spares and repairs from Herberts Cycles, $1/2$ mile from start.
Public transport and bike links: Whitstable station, $3/4$ mile from start. Herne Bay station, 1 mile from finish.
Parking: Paid car parks at start. Free parking at Hampton Pier.
Maps and guides: OS Landranger 179, Explorer 150.
Website: www.sustrans.org.uk/find-a-route-on-the-national-cycle-network/oyster-bay-trail

2. After 1.5 miles, at Long Rock, turn right to follow the concrete track that loops around the outskirts of the nature reserve.

3. Return to the seafront path and follow it to Hampton Pier, on the outskirts of Herne Bay. The route follows roads through Herne Bay.

SOUTHERN COUNTIES

The Viking Coastal Trail: Reculver to Margate Ride 26

The Viking Coastal Trail is the name given to a 32-mile ride around the shoreline of the Isle of Thanet, at the north-eastern tip of the coast of Kent. It is a mixture of traffic-free trails, quiet roads and traffic-calmed streets in the coastal towns. The section from Reculver to Margate is the one with the highest traffic-free proportion. It starts from the distinctive towers of the ruins of St Mary's Church and proceeds east along a wide concrete sea wall, with a shingle beach to your left with many breakwaters made of huge boulders. Away to the right are flat, fertile fields dedicated to arable farming. Coastal resorts at Birchington and Westgate are interspersed with sandy bays. Shingle beaches turn to low chalk cliffs and before long you can sample the delights of Margate.

On your bikes!

1. The route is signposted as the 'Viking Trail' from Reculver on a wide concrete path along the sea wall.

2. After almost 4 miles, this first traffic-free section ends in a car park near Minnis Bay. Go around the edge of the car park, descend to the promenade and turn right (follow signs).

3. Go past a series of low chalk cliffs. Almost 2 miles after the car park and about 200m before the end of the path (there are steps ahead with railings), keep an eye out for a right turn uphill on a cobbled path cut through the chalk.

4. Follow the cycle lane on the road for almost 1 mile then descend back down to the promenade. Dismount in front of the beach huts as indicated by the signs.

5. The trail leads into the heart of Margate where you may turn around after finding some refreshments or continue along the Viking Coastal Trail (which has more road sections beyond this point) to North Foreland, Broadstairs and Ramsgate.

Refreshments: King Ethelbert Inn, Reculver. Lots of choice from Minnis Bay eastwards to Margate.
Bike hire and repairs: VCT Bike Hire at Honey'z Cafe, Minnis Bay. Several bike shops in Margate.
Public transport and bike links: Margate station, 200m from seafront. Birchington station, 5 miles from start.
Parking: Paid car park at start, Reculver Country Park. Paid car parks near Margate seafront/town centre.
Maps and guides: OS Landranger 179, Explorer 150.
Website: *explorekent.org/activities/viking-coastal-trail*

Start
Reculver Country Park, near the King Ethelbert Inn (51.3793, 1.1982, TR 227693)

Finish
Margate, Kent (51.3872, 1.3784, TR 352708)

Distance
9 miles/14.5km.

Category
Seafront promenades.

Other facilities

NB *In the Margate area there are several short sections where cyclists must dismount in front of the rows of beach huts between 10 a.m. to 6 p.m. from May to September. Young children might easily run out of the huts or cross without looking from the beach back to the huts, hence the need for this measure.*

47

Traffic-Free Cycle Trails South East England

Western Counties

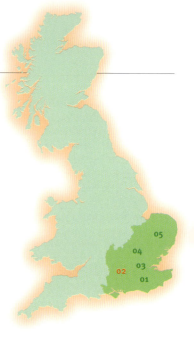

1. Tennyson Trail, Isle of Wight
2. Newport to Sandown, Isle of Wight
3. Newport to Cowes Cycleway, Isle of Wight
4. New Forest, Hampshire
5. Hayling Billy Cycle Trail
6. Staunton Country Park
7. Queen Elizabeth Country Park, Petersfield
8. Meon Valley Trail
9. Cheesefoot Head
10. Mottisfont Abbey
11. Test Way, Stockbridge
12. Watership Down
13. Kennet & Avon Canal through Newbury
14. Alice Holt Forest
15. Basingstoke Canal: Odiham to Fleet
16. Basingstoke Canal: Fleet to the canal centre at Mytchett
17. Blackwater Valley
18. The Look Out, Bracknell Forest/Swinley Forest
19. Kennet & Avon Canal: Reading to Thatcham
20. Reading, along the Thames to Sonning
21. Windsor Great Park
22. Jubilee River Trail
23. Judges Ride
24. Christmas Common to Stonor
25. Thames through Oxford
26. Phoenix Trail: Thame to Princes Risborough
27. Oxford Canal: Heyford to Oxford

Western Counties

02

Western Counties

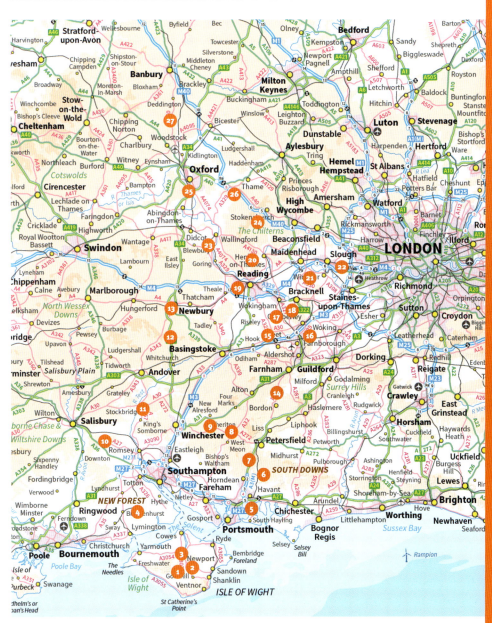

CONTAINS ORDNANCE SURVEY DATA © CROWN COPYRIGHT AND DATABASE RIGHT

49

Ride 1 Tennyson Trail
Isle of Wight

Start
Down Lane,
Carisbrooke
(50.6907, -1.3193,
SZ 481881)

Finish
Freshwater Bay,
Freshwater
(50.6705, -1.5102,
SZ 347817)

Distance
10 miles/16km.

Category
Chalk trails,
byways,
bridleways.

Other facilities

The Isle of Wight is an ideal holiday destination for cyclists, with miles of good bridleway, quiet roads and coast-to-coast trails. The Tennyson Trail is a long-distance walking route on the western side of the island, running from Carisbrooke to The Needles, much of it on bridleways. The high chalk trail over Brighstone Down is a great mountain or gravel bike route, offering superb views over the Solent and Hampshire coast.

On your bikes!
1. The route begins on Down Lane, off Nodgham Lane, which becomes a sunken lane as it climbs over Bowcombe Down; the trail follows farm tracks and forest trails for 3 miles to reach Brighstone Down.

2. Follow the trail through and around the edge of Brighstone Forest; cross Lynch Lane and continue on over Mottistone Down.

Refreshments: The Eight Bells pub, Carisbrooke. The Piano Cafe, Albion Hotel and Dimbola Tea Room in Freshwater Bay.
Bike hire and repairs: Hire, spares and repairs from Adrian's Bike Shop, Freshwater Bay. More choice in Newport.
Public transport and bike links: Red Squirrel Trail can also be followed from Newport, 1.5 miles from start, to Cowes (ferry port).
Parking: Paid car parks at Castle and High Street, Carisbrooke. Paid car parks at Freshwater Bay.
Maps and guides: OS Landranger 196, Explorer OL29.

3. The trail continues in a gentle descent on chalk tracks over Compton Down and across a golf course; there is a final steep descent into Freshwater Bay.

50

WESTERN COUNTIES

Newport to Sandown Isle of Wight Ride 2

This ride forms part of what might be considered the easiest coast-to-coast ride in the country: from Cowes on the north coast of the Isle of Wight to Sandown on the east coast. The section from Newport to Cowes is described in the next ride. The middle section is a complicated route on streets through Newport. The final part, described here, follows a railway path south and east across the island through rich agricultural land and clumps of broadleaf woodland, to arrive in Sandown for a chance to paddle in the sea.

On your bikes!

1. The trail begins on the outskirts of Newport, at the end of Shide Path. Navigation is straightforward: it follows the straight line of the old railway, and is well waymarked as National Cycle Network (NCN) Route 23. It begins as a tree-lined path beside the River Medina.

2. Near Blackwater, the path veers away from the River Medina; **take care** when crossing the A3020 main road. The route is briefly on access roads for 200m near the old station at Merstone and for another 200m on the approach to the A3056; you should cross the main road using the toucan crossing. Turn right after the crossing and look for the trail forking to the left.

3. The trail follows the course of the River Yar, crossing three quiet roads, to reach the outskirts of the seaside town of Sandown.

Refreshments: Plenty of choice in Sandown and Newport. Pedallers Cafe on the trail near Newchurch.
Bike hire and repairs: Several bike shops in Newport. Spares and repairs from Al's Bikes, Sandown.
Public transport and bike links: Sandown rail station, $1/2$ mile from trail end (Ryde to Shanklin line). Red Squirrel Trail can also be followed from Newport to Cowes (ferry port).
Parking: Paid car parks in Newport centre. Paid car parks in Sandown town centre. Car park at trail start and Merstone station.
Maps and guides: OS Landranger 196, Explorer OL29.
Website: www.redsquirreltrail.org.uk

Start
Shide Path, Newport, near junction of A3020 and B3041 (50.6912, -1.2884, SZ 504882)

Finish
Perowne Way, Sandown (50.6610, -1.1613, SZ 594849)

Distance
8 miles/13km.

Category
Railway paths.

Other facilities

51

Ride 3 Newport to Cowes Cycleway Isle of Wight

Start: The Guildhall, Newport (50.7004, -1.2933, SZ 500892)

Finish: Arctic Road, Medina Court industrial estate, Cowes (50.7502, -1.2954, SZ 498947)

Distance: 4 miles/6.5km.

Category: Railway paths.

Other facilities:

The Isle of Wight is a great place to explore by bike and as taking a car on the ferry is so expensive, it is well worth leaving the car on the mainland and catching the ferry with just your bikes. In this way you will also avoid adding to the vehicle traffic on the island. This ride from Cowes to Newport is one of four railway paths on the Isle of Wight. The three others run from Freshwater to Yarmouth, from Shanklin railway station to Wroxall and south-east from Newport to Sandown (see p51). The Cowes to Newport Cycleway runs for four miles alongside the River Medina, a wide expanse of water with hundreds of moored yachts. Cowes is of course a famous yachting centre, and during Cowes Week the whole of the Solent is filled with bright sails.

On your bikes!

1. From the Guildhall/clock tower in the centre of Newport, turn along Quay Street. Follow round a sharp left-hand bend then turn second right on to Little London, signposted 'Cowes Bike Route'.

2. Follow this road around a left-hand bend. At the T-junction at the end of

Refreshments: Plenty of choice in Newport and Cowes.

Bike hire and repairs: Mountain bike hire from Two Elements, Cowes. Hire, spares and repairs from Adrian's Bike Shop, 200m from trail end. Several bike shops in Newport, including Isle of Wight bikes 50m from clock tower.

Public transport and bike links: Ferry port, 1 mile from trail end.

Parking: Paid car parks in Newport centre. Paid car park at Medina Riverside Park. Somerton (paid) car park near trail end.

Maps and guides: OS Landranger 196, Explorer OL29.

Website: www.redsquirreltrail.org.uk

Hurstake Road, turn right, signposted 'Cowes'. Continue straight ahead at the roundabout on to Manners View, passing a large Royal Mail building.

3. Join the trail proper. Follow for 4 miles alongside the River Medina.

4. The trail ends in Cowes at the Medina Court industrial estate, Arctic Road.

New Forest Hampshire — Ride 4

The New Forest's gravel forest tracks link villages and the main tourist sites. The vast majority of the tracks and trails lie either side of an imaginary line drawn between Beaulieu in the south-east and Fordingbridge in the north-west, passing through Bolderwood. The A31 can be crossed via an underpass near to Bolderwood. Great care should be taken crossing roads in the New Forest as many can get busy, especially at the weekends and through the summer holidays. The Hawkhill Trail is described below, but there are over 100 miles of waymarked routes. You are encouraged to make up your own routes, as long as you stay on the gravel tracks waymarked with green and white disks.

On your bikes!

1. Leave the Roundhill Campsite via the access road, cross the B3055 **with care** (this is a busy road) and continue straight on, ignoring junctions to the left and right. Cross over the railway using the bridge.

2. Continue on, through several gates, past waymarker 303. Continue straight on, at a track crossroads, on to a wooded trail. At a T-junction (waymarker 286), turn right. Fork right near waymarker 285.

3. Pass through a conifer plantation, and turn right on to a tarmac road (waymarker 296). Take the left fork at waymarker 297. Continue straight on, crossing the railway line again. Shortly after the railway junction, turn left at the junction and continue straight on, across a cattle grid.

4. Turn right at the junction by waymarker 330. Continue straight on, through two sets of gates. Turn left at the crossroads (waymarker 332). Make a sharp right near waymarker 337.

5. Continue straight on to reach the car park at Beaulieu Heath (a good alternative starting point, if you are driving to the trail).

6. Cross the road **with care**; continue straight on and then turn right at a T-junction. You are now on the old airfield perimeter road. After a left-hand bend, turn right at waymarker 318. After a short distance, take the left turn at waymarker 317 (this is easily missed). Continue straight on to return to Roundhill Campsite.

Refreshments: Lots of choice in Brockenhurst and Lyndhurst.

Bike hire and repairs: Spares, repairs and hire from Cyclexperience Bike Hire, Brockenhurst and The Woods Cyclery (with cafe), Lyndhurst; other cycle hire options elsewhere in the New Forest.

Public transport and bike links: Brockenhurst station, 2.5 miles and Beaulieu Road station, 1 mile from route, via National Cycle Network (NCN) Route 2 (partially en route). New Forest Tour bus (free bike carriage, space for up to 3 on each bus) links route to Brockenhurst and Beaulieu Road stations, as well as Lyndhurst.

Parking: Parking en route at Beaulieu Heath; other car parks close to route at Tilery Road and Matley Wood; 100 car parks in New Forest, all free.

Maps and guides: OS Landranger 195 & 196, Explorer OL22.

Website: www.forestryengland.uk/new-forest

Start/finish
Roundhill Campsite, near Brockenhurst (50.8167, -1.5289, SU 333020)

Distance
9 miles/14.5km.

Category
Wide, gravel forestry tracks.

Other facilities

Ride 5 Hayling Billy Cycle Trail

Start
Near Langstone Bridge, north of Hayling Island (50.8302, -0.9796, SU 720039)

Finish
West Town, Hayling Island (50.7928, -0.9952, SZ 709997)

Distance
3 miles/5km.

Category
Railway paths.

Other facilities

Hayling Island is a small island off the coast of Hampshire, near Havant. A popular sporting destination, it is where a 12-year-old boy, Peter Chilvers, invented the first windsurfing board. The Hayling Island branch line once connected the island with Havant but was a victim of Beeching cuts, and now a traffic-free cycle ride runs north to south along the west coast of the island. The 2.5-mile-long trail is the perfect family day out. If you want a longer route, the 15-mile Langstone Harbour route takes advantage of National Cycle Network (NCN) routes 22 and 222 to travel down the island, cross to Southsea on the outskirts of Portsmouth with your bike on the Hayling ferry and then complete a loop around the harbour on largely off-road cycle trails.

Refreshments: Ship Inn, on other side of Langstone Bridge. Lots of choice in West Town.
Bike hire and repairs: Black Point Cycle Hire, Sandy Point, Hayling Island. Spares and repairs from Hayling Cycles, South Hayling. Lots of bike shops in Southsea/Portsmouth.
Public transport and bike links: Havant station, 2.5 miles from start. NCN 2 offers almost entirely traffic-free route from island to station.
Parking: Free car parks near the start and end of trail, and along the route.
Maps and guides: OS Landranger 197 & 196, Explorer OL8.
Website: *haylingbillyheritage.org*

On your bikes!

1. The trail begins at the north end of the island; the island is linked to the mainland by the A3023 main road, which has a segregated cycle path running alongside it.

2. It is straightforward to follow the well-surfaced trail for 2.5 miles to West Town – there are no roads to cross. After exploring West Town, you can either return along the Hayling Billy Cycle Trail or take to the roads for 1.5 miles to reach the Hayling ferry and continue on the Langstone Harbour loop.

© SUE UNDERWOOD, CYCLE HAYLING

WESTERN COUNTIES

Staunton Country Park Ride 6

Staunton Country Park is a country estate north-east of Portsmouth that was first landscaped in the Regency period. The park is famous for its follies. The green mountain bike trail is a 5.5-mile loop, which does have a short stretch on quiet roads. If you want to avoid traffic entirely, you can take a shortcut on the bridleway to complete the loop off-road or ride the shorter Havant Thicket Boundary trail (2.5 miles). The estate was once owned by George Staunton, the son of the East Indian botanist (another George Staunton) who reputedly first brought Earl Grey tea back from China, so it only makes sense to round off your visit with a trip to the estate's Regency Tea Rooms.

On your bikes!

1. The trail starts on Middle Park Way, 50m west of the entrance to Staunton Farm; follow the track into the country park. Continue straight on for 300m, ignoring tracks to the left (towards the lake) and right (to the tea room).

2. Continue on the track as it bends sharply to the right. Follow the track into the woods, ignoring walking trails to the right and left.

3. Follow the trail towards the edge of the park. Near houses, the track bends in a semicircle and shortly after joins a bridleway. You should fork right to stay on the trail rather than follow the bridleway.

4. You pass Havant Thicket car park where the shorter Havant Thicket Boundary trail begins. Continue straight on.

5. At a trail T-junction, turn right and at the edge of the park, turn left. Follow the trail around the edge of the thicket to a dog-leg. Continue around the edge of the thicket. If you wish to ride the shorter Havant Thicket Boundary trail, turn left $3/4$ mile after the dog-leg bend. Otherwise continue straight on.

6. 600m after the Havant Thicket junction, you reach the bridleway – if you wish to avoid roads, turn left on to the bridleway; this will return you to the green mountain bike trail (end of step 3); retrace your route back to the car park. To remain on the trail continue straight on, across the bridleway.

7. After 500m, turn right and then left on to Swanmore Road. At a T-junction, turn left on to Middle Park Way to return to the start.

Refreshments: Regency Tea Rooms in Staunton Country Park; cafe at Staunton Farm.
Bike hire and repairs: Evans and Halfords in Havant, more choice in Portsmouth.
Public transport and bike links:
1.5 miles from Bedhampton and Havant stations on National Cycle Network (NCN) Route 22 (largely off-road).
Parking: Paid parking at start.
Maps and guides: OS Landranger 197, Explorer OL8.
Website: *www.hants.gov.uk/thingstodo/countryparks/staunton-country-park*

Start/finish
Middle Park Way entrance to Staunton Country Park (50.8739, -0.9758, SU 722088)

Distance
5.5 miles/9km.

Category
Hard-surfaced trails, quiet country lanes (alternative bridleway route).

Other facilities

Ride 7 Queen Elizabeth Country Park Petersfield

Start/finish
Visitor centre, Queen Elizabeth Country Park (50.9614, -0.9783, SU 718185)

Distance
4 miles/6km (family/blue-grade trail); 4.5 miles/7km (mountain bike/red-grade trail).

Category
Forest trails.

Other facilities

Queen Elizabeth Country Park is certainly not flat, but there is an excellent waymarked woodland circuit (purple waymarks) as well as plenty of other attractions in the park and at the visitor centre. For the more adventurous there is a technically challenging mountain bike circuit (orange waymarks). There are also trails leading out of the park on to the network of bridleways and lanes that criss-cross the South Downs, the great chalk ridge stretching from Winchester to Eastbourne. The park is in the South Downs National Park. Queen Elizabeth Country Park covers 1,400 acres and is dominated by the three hills of Butser, War Down and Holt Down, which provide a contrast between the dramatic downland and beautiful woodland. With 38 species of butterfly and 12 species of wild orchid, it is a naturalist's paradise, a large area of which is designated as a Site of Special Scientific Interest. The many Roman and Iron Age sites in the park are also preserved as scheduled ancient monuments.

Refreshments: Cafe at visitor centre.
Bike hire and repairs: Southern Ebike Rentals in the park.
Public transport and bike links: Petersfield rail station, 4.5 miles from Queen Elizabeth Country Park via South Downs Way long-distance bridleway, which passes through park.
Parking: Paid car park by visitor centre.
Maps and guides: OS Landranger 197, Explorer OL33.
Website: *www.forestryengland.uk/queen-elizabeth-country-park*

On your bikes!

1. The routes are well signposted. The trails start from the corner of the car park to the left of the visitor centre by a large, colourful, wooden signpost, or alternatively go through the first car park and on to the Gravel Hill car park. In general terms, the purple (easier) route climbs steadily for the first half of the route and descends for the second half.

WESTERN COUNTIES

Meon Valley Trail Ride 8

If you don't want to tackle the lumps and bumps of the South Downs, the Meon Valley Trail offers a flat and wide track through southern farmlands. This gentle trail on a disused railway meanders between villages, so there are plenty of opportunities for a refreshment break. For visitors wanting a longer expedition, the route crosses the South Downs Way long-distance trail near Exton.

On your bikes!

1. The trail leaves from Station Road, on the outskirts of West Meon. It follows the course of the old railway, generally passing under roads.

2. The trail continues on past Wickham, but to progress further, you will have to negotiate roads.

Refreshments: Plenty of choice along the Meon Valley, including the Shoe Inn, Exton; The Bucks Head, Corhampton; The White Lion, Soberton; Greens Restaurant and Bar, Wickham.
Public transport and bike links: Fareham station, 4 miles from Wickham.
Parking: Free Meon Valley Trail car park at start. Free Wickham car park at end.
Maps and guides: OS Landranger 185 & 196, Explorer OL3.
Website: www.hants.gov.uk/thingstodo/countryside/finder/meonvalleytrail

Start
Station Road, West Meon (51.0102, -1.0876, SU 641238)

Finish
Fareham Road, Wickham (50.8974, -1.1869, SU 572111)

Distance
9.5 miles/15.5km.

Category
Railway paths.

Other facilities

© SIT AND TAKE IN THE VIEW

57

Ride 9 Cheesefoot Head

Start
A272, Cheesefoot Head (51.0469, -1.2474, SU 528277)

Finish
B3046, Cheriton (51.0539, -1.1709, SU 582286)

Distance
4 miles/6.5km.

Category
Chalk-topped bridleways.

Other facilities
P X ~

The scenic natural amphitheatre of Cheesefoot Head, just outside Winchester, is more peaceful now than it was in June 1944, when General Eisenhower addressed the American troops stationed here before D-Day. This route follows a section of the South Downs Way; the Way can be followed to its start in Winchester. The trail ends in the charming village of Cheriton, with its two pubs, including the Flower Pots Inn with its own microbrewery.

On your bikes!

1. The trail starts where the South Downs Way crosses the A272; follow the Way past Cheesefoot Head and turn right at Keeper's Cottage. After just over 1 mile turn left on Honey Lane.

2. Turn right at track T-junction; follow the track as it becomes an access road for 1 mile into Cheriton village.

Refreshments: Flower Pots Inn and Hinton Arms pubs in Cheriton.
Bike hire and repairs: Bike hire from Bespoke Biking, Winchester, 4 miles from start. Ebike hire from the Cycle Company, Shawford, 4 miles from start. Several bike shops in Winchester.
Public transport and bike links: Shawford station, 4 miles from start; Winchester rail station, 4 miles (via South Downs Way, on- and off-road).
Parking: Small (free) car park at start.
Maps and guides: OS Landranger 185, Explorer OL32.
Website: www.nationaltrail.co.uk/en_GB/trails/south-downs-way

© SEAN HOWELL, MARMALADE MTB

WESTERN COUNTIES

Mottisfont Abbey Ride 10

Mottisfont Abbey is a National Trust property on the River Test. There is a museum at the house and a walled garden, as well as family friendly cycling routes around the pretty estate. There is a charge to visit the estate, so these rides are perhaps best as part of a family day out, enjoying all that the grounds have to offer. There are two trails to choose from, the first is 1.5 miles (yellow) and the second is 2.5 miles (red), and an easy link between them; the longer route has some sections on quiet roads, which can be avoided by retracing your tracks.

On your bikes!

1. The red route begins near the junction of Mottisfont Lane and Benger's Lane; turn right on to the bridleway. Follow it for just over $^1/_2$ mile to a road.

2. Continue straight on for 650m; shortly after Cadbury Farm, turn right. You are now on the link between the red and yellow trails. After 500m, continue straight on, now on the yellow route.

3. Continue to follow the yellow route as it bends right. Just before reaching the road turn right towards Spearywell car park. Near the car park, turn right to return to the link route between yellow and red routes.

4. Turn right on the link route. There are some short sections on quiet roads on the rest of the yellow route – these can be avoided by turning left when you reach the red route to retrace your track to the start. Otherwise to complete the red route, continue straight on to a zigzag track through woods.

5. When the track reaches Spearywell Road, turn right. At Hatt Hill, turn left on to the Test Way to return to the start.

Refreshments: Two National Trust cafes near start.
Public transport and bike links: Mottisfont and Dunbridge station, $^3/_4$ mile from start. National Cycle Network (NCN) routes 24 and 246 run through Mottisfont.
Parking: National Trust car park near start, included in admission.
Maps and guides: OS Landranger 185, Explorer 131.
Website: www.nationaltrust.org.uk/mottisfont

Start/finish
Benger's Lane, Mottisfont
(51.0410, -1.5398, SU 324270)

Distance
4.5 miles/7km.

Category
Multi-use tracks, estate roads.

Other facilities

TRAFFIC-FREE CYCLE TRAILS SOUTH EAST ENGLAND

Ride 11 Test Way Stockbridge

Start
Trafalgar Way, Stockbridge
(51.1126, -1.4892, SU 358349)

Finish
Test Way car park, Stonymarsh
(51.0406, -1.5233, SU 335269)

Distance
5 miles/8km.

Category
Railway paths.

Other facilities

This five-mile section of the Test Way runs south from the large, attractive village of Stockbridge, parallel with and occasionally crossing the delightfully clear, shallow, fast-flowing River Test, one of the best fishing rivers in England. The old railway track has been converted into a good, stone-based trail. There is a traffic-free connection from the end of the railway path to the lane leading to Mottisfont Abbey, a National Trust property with a tea room. The Test Valley railway line was also known as the 'Sprat & Winkle Line'. It was unusual in that it was built on the bed of an old canal that linked Andover and Southampton. The waterway was first used in 1794 but had fallen into disuse within 50 years. The railway began service in 1865 and was used in both world wars to move troops and supplies to Southampton Docks. It closed in 1964 and has since become part of the Test Way, a long-distance footpath from Inkpen to Totton. Short sections of it are also open to cyclists.

On your bikes!

1. Join the Test Way by the White Hart on the A30 roundabout in Stockbridge.

Refreshments: Lots of choice in Stockbridge. The John O'Gaunt pub by the River Test at Horsebridge. Tea room at Mottisfont Abbey, a National Trust property.

Public transport and bike links: Mottisfont and Dunbridge station, $3/4$ mile from start. National Cycle Network (NCN) routes 24 and 246 run through Mottisfont.

Parking: Paid Lion's Den car park, Cow Drove Hill Lane, near Stockbridge. Free Test Way car park, Stonymarsh.

Maps and guides: OS Landranger 185, Explorer 131.

Website: www.hants.gov.uk/thingstodo/countryside/cycling/testway

Continue to follow the railway path to the car park at Stonymarsh.

2. If you want to visit Mottisfont Abbey, continue straight on, on the shared-use path beside the A3057. Turn right on to Mottisfont Lane; this is a narrow country lane and may be busy with visitors to the National Trust property.

60

WESTERN COUNTIES

Watership Down Ride 12

Watership Down is part of the North Wessex Downs Area of Natural Beauty; long an area associated with horse racing, the Downs are criss-crossed with bridleways that make for a great, if hilly, gravel bike adventure. Richard Adams, author of *Watership Down*, lived in the nearby town of Whitchurch. The narrow lane out of Litchfield is the access road for a handful of houses, so you may encounter occasional traffic on the very start of this trail.

On your bikes!

1. Follow the tarmac track east out of the village; after 1.5 miles, at a track crossroads, turn right. At a T-junction, turn left; after 1.5 miles, turn left to climb to Watership Down.

2. Follow the now stone-topped track as it bends right across the top of Watership Down; continue on to White Hill. Cross the road **with care** and continue straight on, via the car park access road, to a muddy, hedge-lined trail. Cross Meadham Lane and continue straight on, on the tarmac bridleway. At a track T-junction, turn left to reach North Oakley.

Refreshments: Nothing en route; the Vine pub at Hannington, 1 mile from end.
Bike hire and repairs: Nearest hire, spares and repairs are Basingstoke, 8 miles from end.
Public transport and bike links: Whitchurch station, 3.5 miles (on-road) from start. Overton station, 3 miles from end.
Parking: Free car park at White Hill (middle of trail).
Maps and guides: OS Landranger 174 & 185, Explorer 144.

Start
Litchfield road, Litchfield
(51.2822, -1.3395, SU 461538)

Finish
Near Manor Farm, North Oakley
(51.2828, -1.2328, SU 536540)

Distance
8.5 miles/13.5km.

Category
Tarmac lanes, grass- and stone-topped bridleways, muddy trails.

Other facilities

61

TRAFFIC-FREE CYCLE TRAILS SOUTH EAST ENGLAND

Ride 13 Kennet & Avon Canal through Newbury

Start
Bridge Street, Newbury (51.4019, -1.3243, SU 471672)

Finish
Thatcham station, Thatcham (51.3935, -1.2436, SU 527663)

Distance
7 miles/11.5km.

Category
Canal towpaths.

Other facilities

On its way from Bath to Reading, National Cycle Network (NCN) Route 4 diverges from the Kennet & Avon Canal towpath from Devizes through Hungerford to a few miles west of Newbury: there is an excellent network of quiet lanes which offers safe and attractive cycling. The towpath is rejoined three miles west of Newbury at Hamstead Park, giving cyclists a fine entry into (or exit from) the centre of Newbury. The orange, sandy path passes a series of pillboxes built as a line of defence during World War II and runs underneath the Newbury A34 bypass. The path crosses Bridge Street in the centre of Newbury and continues eastwards alongside the canal to Thatcham. The next section (from Reading to Thatcham) is described on p68. Mountain or gravel bikes are recommended. There are chicane barriers on this route.

On your bikes!

1. The canal towpath can be reached by following the brick track besides Costa on Bridge Street. After the bridge under the A339 main road, the cycle path follows the right fork.

Refreshments: Lots of choice in Newbury.
Bike hire and repairs: Spares and repairs from ChainWorx in Newbury.
Public transport and bike links: Newbury station, $1/2$ mile from start. Thatcham station, end of route. NCN 4 can be followed along canal into Reading.
Parking: Paid town centre car parks near start. Paid parking at Thatcham station.
Maps and guides: OS Landranger 174, Explorer 158.
Website: www.sustrans.org.uk/find-a-route-on-the-national-cycle-network/kennet-and-avon-cycle-route

2. Just before Ham Lock, cross the canal to follow the towpath on the southern side. Take the ramp to the road, cross the road and turn left to follow NCN 4 on the shared-use path beside the B3421.

3. Turn right to follow the shared-use path along Lower Way. Continue on the shared-use path into Thatcham town centre; if you want to continue on to Reading on NCN 4, there is a short on-road section in Thatcham.

WESTERN COUNTIES

Alice Holt Forest Ride 14

These two easy, well-designed routes on the sandy soils south of Farnham, part of the greensand strata that runs east from Alton between the chalk of the North Downs and the clay of the Weald, provide all-year-round tracks. The well-waymarked, circular route starts from the visitor centre and uses stone and gravel paths with the occasional gentle hill. The Shipwrights Way is a linear route, part of a longer 50-mile route going to Portsmouth. From the Middle Ages onwards, timber from Alice Holt was being used to build ships for Britain's navy. Hundreds of mature oaks were needed to build a single ship and the forest was stripped of its large trees to supply the naval shipyards dotted along the south coast.

On your bikes!

1. The Family Trail is a 3-mile gravel loop around the forest that has blue waymarks. Take care on the long descent near the start.

2. The Shipwrights Way is a 50-mile trail from Bentley to Portsmouth, following the route of the timber to the dockyards. It runs north-west from the visitor centre towards Bentley railway station, through the woods, and also south from the visitor centre to the Cradle Lane bridleway.

Refreshments: Cafe at the visitor centre.
Bike hire and repairs: Cycle hire from Alice Holt Inclusive Cycling; cycle shops in Farnham.
Public transport and bike links: Bentley station, on edge of forest, 2 miles from visitor centre.
Parking: Paid parking at start.
Maps and guides: OS Landranger 186, Explorer 144 & 145, OL33.
Website: *www.forestryengland.uk/alice-holt-forest*

Start/finish
Visitor centre, Alice Holt Forest (51.1688, -0.8392, SU 813417)

Distance
3 miles/5km each (Family Trail/Shipwrights Way).

Category
Forestry trails.

Other facilities

63

Ride 15 Basingstoke Canal: Odiham to Fleet

Start
Reading Road bridge, Fleet (51.2762, -0.8418, SU 809536)

Finish
Greywell Tunnel, Odiham (51.2578, -0.9711, SU 719415)

Distance
10 miles/16km.

Category
Canal towpaths.

Other facilities

The Basingstoke Canal runs from near Odiham in Hampshire to the junction with the Wey Navigation near West Byfleet. It has been split into three sections, each about 10 miles long. This westernmost section runs from the Greywell Tunnel, near Odiham, past the ruins of Odiham Castle and on to Fleet. The Basingstoke Canal was completed in 1794. It was 37 miles long with 29 locks and a 1,130-metre tunnel through Greywell Hill. The canal was built to boost agricultural trade in central Hampshire, carrying coal and fertilisers from London and returning with timber, corn and other produce to the capital. The canal was never a commercial success and by the mid-1960s it was lying semi-derelict. All the locks were decaying, the towpath was overgrown and the water channel choked by weed, refuse and silt. Efforts to stop the rot were made by the Surrey & Hampshire Canal Society. Restoration work was completed and the canal reopened in 1991.

On your bikes!
1. Join the canal towpath at Reading Road bridge in the centre of Fleet. Follow the towpath south-west, keeping the water to your left. No instructions

Refreshments: Fox & Hounds pub, just west of Fleet. The Exchequer pub, Crookham Village. Barley Mow pub, Winchfield Hurst. Waterwitch pub, Odiham.
Bike hire and repairs: Spares and repairs from Pedal Heaven and Cycle Science in Fleet.
Public transport and bike links: Fleet station, 1 mile from start. Hook station, 2.5 miles from end. Several other stations along canal.
Parking: Fleet Wharf car park, near junction of B3013 and A323. Also free canalside car parks at Winchfield Hurst (near Barley Mow pub) and Crookham Wharf. Basingstoke Canal (free) car park, Odiham, near Waterwitch pub.
Maps and guides: OS Landranger 186, Explorer 144 & 145.
Website: *basingstoke-canal.org.uk*

are needed as it is very straightforward to follow the canal.

2. After about 9 miles, and shortly after passing the extraordinary ruins of Odiham Castle (on your right), the towpath ends at the portal to Greywell Tunnel.

WESTERN COUNTIES

16

Basingstoke Canal: Ride 16
Fleet to the canal centre at Mytchett

This is the middle section of the Basingstoke Canal, and despite its proximity to the built-up areas along the Blackwater Valley, it has a very green, woodland feel. It starts at the fascinating visitor centre at Mytchett (which also has a tea room for when you get back from your ride), and heads south past Mytchett Lake and Greatbottom Flash. Pass high above the A331 dual carriageway running up the Blackwater Valley and continue across gorse- and heather-covered heathland to Fleet. You may wish to continue further west (previous ride) or indeed from the visitor centre you could just as easily head north then east towards Weybridge (p80). The Basingstoke Canal is thought by many to be Britain's most beautiful waterway. From the rolling hills of North Hampshire to the dramatic flights of locks in Surrey, the tree-lined canal offers a variety of delights, from 200-year-old bridges and locks to traditionally painted narrowboats.

On your bikes!

1. From the Basingstoke Canal Centre at Mytchett cross the bridge over the canal and turn left, keeping the water to your left. Soon go past Mytchett Lake and Greatbottom Flash.

2. Cross the viaduct over the A331 and the River Blackwater. The quality of the towpath deteriorates then improves.

3. Pass through a landscape of heathland and gorse, and beneath two big, black metal 'Meccano'-style bridges.

4. The suggested turnaround point is the centre of Fleet where there is a choice of pubs and cafes, but if you wish to carry on, the canal continues for a further 10 miles to the tunnel at Greywell (previous ride).

Refreshments: Tea room at canal centre at Mytchett. Lots of choice in Fleet.
Bike hire and repairs: Spares and repairs from Pedal Heaven and Cycle Science in Fleet.
Public transport and bike links: North Camp and Ash Vale rail stations, 1.5 miles from start. Fleet station 1 mile from end.
Parking: Fleet Wharf car park, near junction of B3013 and A323.
Maps and guides: OS Landranger 186, Explorer 145.
Website: *basingstoke-canal.org.uk*

Start
Basingstoke Canal Centre, Mytchett (51.2884, -0.7204, SU 893551)

Finish
Reading Road bridge, Fleet (51.2762, -0.8418, SU 809536)

Distance
9 miles/15km.

Category
Canal towpaths.

Other facilities

65

Ride 17 Blackwater Valley

Start
A30 and A331 junction, Blackwater
(51.3317, -0.7749; SU 854598)

Finish
Aldershot College, Aldershot
(51.2428, -0.7171; SU 882500)

Distance
8 miles/13km.

Category
River paths.

Other facilities

The Blackwater Valley is a green haven in this built-up region on the Hampshire–Surrey border. The trail is occasionally narrow, as it is primarily a walking trail; permissive rights to cycle have been granted. The trail is never far from main roads, but it offers a green route on well-surfaced paths with plenty of opportunity for bird spotting, and is a great option for a traffic-free trip because of the railway stations that are dotted along the route.

On your bikes!

1. The trail starts on the A30, near its junction with the A331; follow the trail south. The trail winds through a grassy corridor between the railway and the A331 main road, and passes under the M3 motorway.

2. The trail emerges on to the road; **take care** when crossing Frimley High Street at the crossing point. The route runs alongside Frimley High Street on shared-use path for 250m before forking left towards the banks of the River Blackwater.

3. The trail emerges near the Kingfisher on the Quay pub at Mytchett. Turn right and follow the access road as it curves up to the Coleford Bridge Road.

4. The path by the road is not shared use; you are advised to dismount and turn left to use the pavement to cross two roundabouts straight ahead. The trail is on the left after 250m and runs next to the A331 main road. When the trail runs out, turn left on to the access road for 50m and at the road end, turn right to follow the trail under the bridge. After the bridge turn left to follow the trail south, keeping the lake to your right.

Refreshments: Plenty of choices in Farnborough and Aldershot; Kingfisher on the Quay near Farnborough North.
Bike hire and repairs: Several bike shops in Farnborough, including Spokes & Spanners, and Silvester Brothers Cycles.
Public transport and bike links: Blackwater station at start. Ash station, 1 mile from end. Frimley, Farnborough Green, Farnborough North, North Camp stations en route.
Parking: Free Hawley Meadows car park, 1/2 mile from start (en route). Limited on-street parking near end.
Maps and guides: OS Landranger 186, Explorer 145.
Website: www.hants.gov.uk/thingstodo/countryside/cycling/blackwatervalley

5. Follow the trail under the railway and over the railway to enter Lakeside Park Nature Reserve; the trail weaves between the lakes. With the river, take the Ash Aqueduct over the A331 main road.

6. Descend from the A311 main road and follow the River Blackwater. The trail finishes near Aldershot College on the outskirts of Aldershot.

66

WESTERN COUNTIES

The Look Out Ride 18
Bracknell Forest/Swinley Forest

This area of the Crown Estate comprises 2,600 acres of predominantly Scots Pine woodland. The current policy is to increase the amount of broadleaf trees where appropriate. Although owned and managed by the Crown Estate Commissioners, The Look Out has been set up in partnership with the Bracknell Forest Council. From The Look Out, rides and tracks radiate through the forest. The waymarked rides suggested here are among many that could be devised along the tracks that criss-cross the woodland; you can choose from wide gravel tracks to firm trails to technical singletrack. There is a designated mountain bike area with tricky, testing singletrack, should you be looking for something more challenging. The Discovery Centre at The Look Out is a hands-on science fun centre with over 90 activities.

On your bikes!
There are three waymarked trails:
1. The Green Trail is a $1/2$-mile track on wider trails, although still often singletrack, suitable for new riders and children, with limited ascent and descent.

2. The Blue Trail is a 5.5-mile singletrack route with moderate ascents and descents. Although the surface is generally firm, there are some rocks, roots and muddy sections. It is a great trail for intermediate riders seeking to consolidate experience.

3. The start of the Red Trail overlaps the Blue Trail, so you can warm up and decide whether to tackle the steep ascents and descents, sharp twists and drops and berms of the technical 8.5-mile Red Trail. This trail is suitable for experienced mountain bikers.

Refreshments: Cafe at start.
Bike hire and repairs: Hire from Swinley Bike Hub at start, plenty of bike shops in Bracknell.
Public transport and bike links: Bracknell and Martins Heron stations, 2 miles from start; traffic-free routes into town centre.
Parking: Paid parking at start.
Maps and guides: OS Landranger 175, Explorer 160.
Website: *www.swinleybikehub.com/trails*

Start/finish
Look Out Discovery Centre, Swinley Forest (51.3873, -0.7410, SU 877661)

Distance
$1/2$ mile/1km to 8.5 miles/13.5km.

Category
Forest trails, singletrack.

Other facilities

67

Ride 19 Kennet & Avon Canal: Reading to Thatcham

Start
The Oracle Centre, Reading (51.4524, -0.9723, SU 715731)

Finish
Thatcham station, Thatcham (51.3935, -1.2436, SU 527663)

Distance
16 miles/26km.

Category
Canal towpaths.

Other facilities

Forming part of National Cycle Network (NCN) Route 4 between Bristol and London, the Kennet & Avon Canal towpath between Thatcham and Reading has been improved to a standard suitable for recreational cycling. Although the towpath is predominantly of stone and gravel, there is a 1-mile section that runs along the meadows by the canal, to the east of Aldermaston. There are several pubs along the way and a chance for tea and coffee at Aldermaston Wharf. It is in Reading that the canal links up with the Thames.

On your bikes!

1. There are two cycle-route options to the south of Reading from the Oracle Centre. Either follow Fobney Street and signs for 'Green Park' and 'Majedski Stadium', soon joining the canal towpath on the west side of the canal, **OR** follow 'National Cycle Network Route 4' signs which link cycle paths and quiet streets to the towpath running down the east side of the canal. Both link at the junction of the A33 and Rose Kiln Lane, to the south of Reading (near Whitley); from there turn west towards Theale.

2. There is a short section near to Burghfield Mill where National Cycle

Refreshments: Lots of choice in Reading. Teas and coffees at the visitor centre at Aldermaston Wharf. The Rowbarge Pub, just south of Woolhampton.
Bike hire and repairs: Brompton Bike Hire, Reading station; plenty of bike shops in Reading.
Public transport and bike links: Reading station, 500m from start. Route follows NCN 4 which links London to Wales. Thatcham station is on the canal towpath.
Parking: Paid parking near the Oracle; parking en route at Sheffield Bottom Lock (free), Tyle Mill (paid) and Aldermaston Wharf (paid). Paid parking at Thatcham station.
Maps and guides: OS Landranger 174 & 175, Explorer 158 & 159.
Website: www.sustrans.org.uk/find-a-route-on-the-national-cycle-network/kennet-and-avon-cycle-route

Network Route 4 signs will direct you away from the canal and around the edge of a lake, close to the M4. You rejoin the towpath to the east of Theale (just east of where the M4 bridge crosses the canal).

Reading along the Thames to Sonning Ride 20

Maybe some time in the future there will be a path alongside the whole length of the River Thames, wide enough and of a good enough quality to cater for cyclists and walkers alike. Sadly, at present there are few stretches of the river west of London where it is possible to ride – this section in and near Reading is one of the exceptions. Reading is where the Kennet & Avon Canal, which starts in Bath, joins the Thames, linking Bristol (via the River Avon) to London (via the Thames). It is possible to cycle along the towpath of the canal through Reading and beyond towards Newbury. The town is at an important junction of the National Cycle Network (NCN): Route 4 runs through Reading on its way from London to Wales, and Route 5 heads north from Reading through the Chiltern Hills to Oxford. You will see one of the attractive Sustrans's Millennium Mileposts at the point where Route 4 joins the Thames. Sonning is a fine little village with a good pub.

On your bikes!

1. Access to the riverside path at Reading Bridge is via steps; there is step-free access via nearby King's Meadow Road. Turn right to follow the Thames Path/NCN 5 around King's Meadow.

2. Cross over the Kennet & Avon Canal, using the stepped bridge; there is a

bike ramp. After the bridge, turn left to remain on the Thames Path, now on NCN 4. Just after the rowing club, fork right to follow NCN 4 to the shared-use pavement along Thames Valley Park.

3. After ½ mile turn left off the roundabout by the Thames Valley Park Security building on to the drive towards the David Lloyd fitness centre.

4. Pass to the left of the car park and around a metal field gate, signposted 'Authorised vehicles only'. After ½ mile turn right alongside the river.

5. Follow the track by the river for 1 mile. If you want a riverside lunch, you can stop at the Coppa Club by the river at Sonning Bridge. For the Bull Inn, just **before** Sonning Bridge turn right and walk your bikes up past the church into the village.

Refreshments: Plenty of choice in Reading, including Whittington's Tea Barge, on opposite side of Reading Bridge from start. The Bull Inn and Coppa Club in Sonning.

Bike hire and repairs: Brompton Bike Hire, Reading station; plenty of bike shops in Reading.

Public transport and bike links: Reading station, 500m from start. Route follows NCN 4 and NCN 5 (which both link London to Wales).

Parking: Paid parking at King's Meadow at start; other parking en route at Thames Valley Business Park.

Maps and guides: OS Landranger 175, Explorer 158 & 159.

Website: *www.visitthames.co.uk/things-to-do/cycling*

Start
Reading Bridge, Reading (51.4607, -0.9680, SU 718740)

Finish
Sonning Bridge, Sonning (51.4754, -0.9135, SU 756757)

Distance
3 miles/5km.

Category
Riverside paths.

Other facilities

TRAFFIC-FREE CYCLE TRAILS SOUTH EAST ENGLAND

Ride 21 **Windsor Great Park**

Start/finish
Ranger's Gate, Windsor Great Park (51.4518, -0.6286, SU 954734)

Distance
5-mile/8km circuit.

Category
Estate roads.

Other facilities

Although there will be occasional vehicles within Windsor Great Park, it is a very cycle-friendly place and an amazing oasis of tranquility set in the heart of such a built-up area (the M3, M4, M25 and Heathrow are all less than 10 miles away). There is an estate village with a village shop, the fields are ploughed, seeded and harvested and there are woods and lakes as well as a school. The place is free of the creeping urbanisation that blights so much of the area to the west of London. You are allowed on the tarmac roads (and through the big green gates operated by buttons!). Signs will tell you where you cannot go. Polo matches are frequently played here. Windsor Castle was established by William the Conqueror and it is the largest inhabited castle in the world. The enormous round tower has a view over several counties. Savill Garden is famous for its rhododendrons and the Valley Gardens are noted for their heathers. Nearby is the 160-acre lake of Virginia Water.

On your bikes!

1. Use the toucan crossing to cross the busy A332 into the park via Ranger's Gate. At a crossroads after 1/2 mile, go straight ahead, signposted 'York Club'. Shortly at the next crossroads, go straight ahead again (same sign).

2. Climb past York Club to a pink castle on a left-hand bend at the top. Descend, passing a statue of Queen Elizabeth on a horse to your right.

3. At the fork at the bottom of the hill, bear right then go straight ahead at a crossroads by a red-brick house (or turn right along Duke's Lane as far as Prince Consort's Gate to see the magnificent trees).

Refreshments: Pub at Bishop's Gate. Cafe and restaurant at Savill Garden.
Bike hire and repairs: Spares, repairs and hire from the Bike Company and Extreme Motion, Windsor.
Public transport and bike links: Virginia Water and Egham stations, 7.5 miles from start.
Parking: Paid car park by Ranger's Gate/Ranger's Lodge.
Maps and guides: OS Landranger 175, Explorer 160.
Website: www.windsorgreatpark.co.uk

4. At the T-junction after passing the Royal School, at the top of a climb, turn right (not sharp right to Cumberland Lodge) then at the next T-junction turn right (again not Cumberland).

5. Continue straight ahead past Cumberland Lodge then at the end of the polo ground turn left at a 'Guards Polo Club' sign.

6. At the next crossroads turn left, 'No entry for gardens traffic'. Go past the Savill Garden, following signs for 'Bishopgate' on a wide tarmac road, avoiding all 'No cycling' signs.

7. At the T-junction by Cumberland Gate turn right. Ignore left turns. Go past a large pink house, go straight ahead at a crossroads then pass through big gates operated by a button.

8. Go past Long Walk (with views down towards Windsor Castle) and through a second set of gates. Ignore a left turn then at the crossroads shortly after passing Russell's Field Farm on the right, turn right, signposted 'Ranger's Gate exit', to return to the start.

WESTERN COUNTIES

Jubilee River Trail Ride 22

The Jubilee River is a seven-mile channel, constructed in the 1990s to divert water from the River Thames and prevent flooding around Slough and Maidenhead. The hydraulic channel was designed to look like a natural river, and wildlife-rich reed banks, wetlands and woods were created along the banks. A well-surfaced, three-metre-wide, shared-use path runs most of the length of the channel, although there are road crossings to be negotiated and a short road section.

On your bikes!

1. The route begins on Conduit Lane in Ditton Park; the route may only be open during daylight hours. At other times, you will have to detour on roads on the edge of the park.

2. After 1 mile, the route detours around the back of Slough Rugby Club. After 1/2 mile, the trail crosses the M4 motorway and then emerges on to a road (with shared-use pavement); continue on in the same direction. At the main road, take a staggered path straight ahead to The Myrke. The route then follows the road for 50 metres; the road is narrow and often busy, and you may prefer to dismount and use the pavement.

3. After 50 metres, look for the trail turning off to the left to cross the Jubilee River. Follow the river for 800m; cross the A332 main road using the toucan crossing.

4. Continue along the river for three miles, passing under several roads. Cross the B3026 road. After 1/2 mile, the trail passes under the M4 motorway; this crossing may be closed during flooding.

5. Continue along the river for another 1.5 miles, then cross the river to reach the A4 main road on the outskirts of Maidenhead.

Refreshments: Lots of choice in Slough. Pub and cafe in Taplow, at end.
Bike hire and repairs: Bike hire from Extreme Motion, Windsor, 2 miles from route (largely off-road). Several bike shops in Maidenhead, Slough and Windsor.
Public transport and bike links: Langley station, 1.5 miles from Ditton Park. Taplow station, 750m from end. Route is part of 36-mile National Cycle Network (NCN) Route 61 route that links Maidenhead to Hoddesdon.
Parking: Limited on-street parking near start and end; some car parks en route.
Maps and guides: OS Landranger 175, Explorer 160 & 172.
Website: *www.rbwm.gov.uk/home/transport-and-streets/cycling*

Start
Conduit Lane, Slough (51.4936, -0.5569, TQ 003782)

Finish
Bath Road, Maidenhead (51.5230, -0.6926, SU 908813)

Distance
6.5 miles/10.5km.

Category
Compacted trails, tarmac paths.

Other facilities

© PAUL BAKER

Ride 23 Judges Ride

Start/finish
North Stoke Village Hall, North Stoke (51.5722, -1.1211, SU 610863)

Distance
7.5 miles/12km.

Category
Bridleways, some singletrack, quiet country lanes.

Other facilities

The Judges Ride is a mountain bike and horse riding route through the southern Oxfordshire Chilterns. It consists of three connected loops – the route in total is 16 miles long. The longest loop is described below, not only because it has the shortest sections on road but also because it offers an opportunity to ride along the Ridgeway and the Icknield Way. There are three short sections on quiet country lanes on the longest loop and some narrow gateways en route. This is a route best tackled on mountain, gravel or hybrid bikes.

On your bikes!

1. From North Stoke Village Hall, follow the road north and continue straight on as it becomes bridleway; you are on the Ridgeway.

2. Continue straight on, on the road at Mongewell. The official route turns right after 100m but it would be advisable to remain on the road for 250m and then follow it as it bends right; the deviation avoids a 100m walk along the grass verge of the busy A4074 main road.

3. Cross the A4074 **with care** and continue straight on, on the Ridgeway; follow the Ridgeway for 1 mile, cross the road and continue straight on for another 600m.

Refreshments: Plenty of choice in Wallingford, 1.5 miles north of route or Goring, 3 miles south of route.
Bike hire and repairs: Hires, spares and repairs from Rides on Air, Wallingford.
Public transport and bike links: Goring station, 3 miles south of route, mostly on Ridgeway bridleway.
Parking: Very limited on-street parking at start; it may be easier to use paid parking in Wallingford, 1.5 miles north of route.
Maps and guides: OS Landranger 175, Explorer 171.
Website: www.nationaltrail.co.uk/en_GB/trails/the-ridgeway/cycling

4. Turn right on to a country lane and follow it for $1/2$ mile. At a road junction, where the Chilterns Cycleway is signposted straight on, take the rutted bridleway to the right.

5. Keep straight on, on often singletrack bridleway, crossing two minor roads. Cross the busy A4074 **with care**.

6. Cross one more field on bridleway, and then right on to the Icknield Way.

7. The bridleway reaches the B4009 Wallingford Road; if you want to reach Goring railway station, turn left, first on the road, then on the Ridgeway. To stay on the route, continue straight on, now on road.

8. After 500m, turn right and at a T-junction, turn right and then follow the road as it bends left. Where the road bends right, continue straight on, on bridleway that leaves the road to the left to return to North Stoke.

WESTERN COUNTIES

Christmas Common to Stonor
Ride 24

No one is sure how Christmas Common acquired its festive name: it is perhaps because of a historic battle or a preponderance of holly. The circular route, which descends from the attractive Oxfordshire village, passes through beech woods and farmlands on bridleway and restricted byways to reach Stonor Park, with its historic country house and deer park. On dirt and gravel tracks, this is a route for gravel bikes or at least bikes with knobbly tyres. Near Stonor there is a 700-metre section on country lanes, but you can avoid this on foot via a footpath.

On your bikes!

1. The trail begins on Hollandridge Lane, near the Fox & Hounds pub. Hollandridge Lane is an access road for 500m, before becoming a restricted byway. Follow the byway for 2.5 miles to reach the road. If you want to avoid the road section, look out for a footpath that crosses the byway after 2 miles; dismount and turn left on the footpath, pushing your bike for 700m. When the footpath meets a bridleway, turn left (back on your bike).

2. Turn left on to the road; after 400m, turn left on to Balham's Lane. After 350m, turn left on to a bridleway.

3. Follow the bridleway as it winds back to Hollandridge Lane; turn right and retrace your steps to the start.

Refreshments: Fox & Hounds pub, 150m from start. Cafes in Stonor Park. Cafes at Turville Heath, 800m off-route.
Bike hire and repairs: Spares and repairs from Sprocket Science, Watlington, 2 miles from start.
Public transport and bike links: Henley-on-Thames station, 5 miles away from Stonor end of loop.
Parking: Paid parking at Watlington Hill National Trust car park, 750m north of start.
Maps and guides: OS Landranger 175, Explorer 171.
Website: *www.stonor.com/walking-and-cycling*

Start/finish
Hollandridge Lane, Christmas Common (51.6330, -0.9681, SU 715932)

Distance
6 miles/10km.

Category
Bridleways, some singletrack, quiet country lanes.

Other facilities

© TÍMEA KRISTÓF

Ride 25 Thames through Oxford

Start
Redbridge Park & Ride (51.7291, -1.2483, SP 520036) or Folly Bridge, St Aldates, Oxford (51.7459, -1.2562, SP 514055)

Finish
Perch pub, Binsey (51.7650, -1.2877, SP 493076)

Distance
4 miles/6.5km.

Category
Riverside paths.

Other facilities

NB This route is also popular with walkers. Please ride with consideration for other users, let people know you are coming and thank them if they step aside for you. Where the path is narrow, show courtesy by pulling in and letting walkers pass.

Cycling and Oxford have gone together almost since the invention of the bicycle. This ride explores the towpath of the River Thames from the Ring Road in the south, past all the University of Oxford college boathouses, to the Perch pub in Binsey. There are many architectural attractions along the way including the bridge at Iffley Lock and the folly at Folly Bridge. The southern half of this ride overlaps with the National Cycle Network (NCN), which continues south via a purpose-built cycle track alongside the railway on its way towards Radley and Abingdon. It is also possible to cycle alongside the Oxford Canal up through north Oxford, although the towpath is much narrower and rougher than the Thames Towpath.

On your bikes!

1. Exit Redbridge Park & Ride car park via the entrance and turn right along the cycle path (away from Oxford).

Descend through the subway and at the first T-junction, turn left to go through a second subway. At the second T-junction (with metal barriers to your left), turn right and follow the cycle track parallel with the Ring Road.

2. Cross a bridge over a tributary of the Thames then, just before the much larger bridge over the main course of the Thames, turn left downhill, signposted 'National Cycle Network Route 5', then left along the towpath. (**Remember** this point for your return.)

3. Go past the lock, the Isis Farmhouse and past the college boathouses. At the crossroads by Folly Bridge, use the toucan crossing to go straight ahead on to a continuation of the towpath.

4. Walk your bike through Osney Lock. Descend off the towpath on to East Street by the Punter pub and continue

74

Thames through Oxford — Ride 25

WESTERN COUNTIES

in the same direction parallel with the river. As the street swings round to the left, climb the steps up to the Botley Road.

5. Cross to the other side of the road to join a continuation of the towpath (now on the right side of the river). You may prefer to cross the road using the toucan crossings that lie to the east or west of the bridge.

6. Cross a humpbacked metal and wooden bridge and turn left, following the Thames Path. Follow this with water to both the left and right. After $1/2$ mile go straight ahead past the marina and turn left on the bridge across the river.

7. Go past the boatyard then follow the main wide stone track as it swings left away from the river to arrive at the Perch pub.

Refreshments: Lots of choice in Oxford, most of it just off route. Isis Farmhouse by the Thames, just north of ring road. Head of the River pub at Folly Bridge. Punter pub, junction of East Street and South Street. The Perch pub, Binsey.

Bike hire and repairs: Bike hire options in Oxford include Brompton at station, Bainton Bikes, Donkey Bikes and OxonBike docking stations; plenty of bike shops.

Public transport and bike links: Oxford station, 450m from River Thames at Osney Bridge (north of Punter pub).

Parking: Paid car park at Redbridge; car park south of Port Meadow near end. Paid car parks in Oxford, but centre not car friendly.

Maps and guides: OS Landranger 164, Explorer 180.

Website: *www.sustrans.org.uk/find-other-routes/thames-valley*

75

Ride 26 Phoenix Trail: Thame to Princes Risborough

Start
Thame Leisure Centre, Thame
(51.7468, -0.9933, SP 696058)

Finish
Horsenden Lane, Princes Risborough
(51.7201, -0.8551, SP 792030)

Distance
7 miles/11.5km.

Category
Railway paths.

Other facilities

NB There is no parking along Horsenden Lane at the Princes Risborough end of the Phoenix Trail. There is space for a few cars just off the B4009 immediately south of the old green metal railway bridge between Princes Risborough and Chinnor.

A section of the old railway line that used to link Princes Risborough to Oxford has been converted to recreational use and offers a fine, open ride across the Oxfordshire countryside with wide-ranging views to the steep, wooded escarpment of the Chiltern Hills which lie to the south. Red kites have been introduced to this area and you will see many of these majestic birds with their distinctive forked tails as they wheel high above. Some more unusual animals can also be seen along the trail: about halfway along, perched high up on poles, is a set of bizarre metal animal sculptures. This is one of those good 'conversational' rides where the path is wide and has a fine, smooth surface, allowing you to cycle side by side and put the world to rights. The ride is very popular on summer weekends, as is The Three Horseshoes, the only pub along the route. There are chicane barriers and bollards at road crossings.

On your bikes!

1. Pass between the white buildings of the Thame Leisure Centre and the school. Go straight ahead at a mini roundabout, then first left, keeping the leisure centre buildings close by on your right. Follow a tarmac path across the playing field to join the Phoenix Trail. Turn right. (Remember this point for the return trip.)

2. Follow the trail as it swings left (east). Go straight ahead at a crossroads of tracks, signposted 'Towersey 2, Princes Risborough 7, National Cycle Network Route 57'.

3. Use the toucan crossing to cross the busy road by the industrial estate.

4. Go past a wooden 'Clam' sculpture. The Three Horseshoes pub is shortly after this on your left. Go past animal sculptures on the top of tall poles.

5. The railway path itself finishes 2 miles after passing the animals, at the bridge over the busy B4009. You may wish to turn around here if you do not want to go into Princes Risborough.

6. (On to Princes Risborough.) There is a short, rough section then at the T-junction with tarmac by Glebe Cottage, turn right. (Remember this point for the return trip.)

7. Go past the church. At the T-junction at the end of Horsenden Lane, turn left over the railway bridge and immediately left again following the National Cycle Network Route 57 signs into the centre of Princes Risborough. This will involve busier roads (Horsenden Lane, Picts Lane, Station Road, Manor Park Avenue, Stratton Road, Church Street, Market Street).

Refreshments: Lots of choice in Thame and Princes Risborough. The Three Horseshoes pub in Towersey, about 2 miles east of Thame.
Bike hire and repairs: Thame Cycles and Phoenix Cycles, Thame. Risboro' Car & Cycle Parts, Princes Risborough.
Public transport and bike links: Princes Risborough station, 1.5 miles from end of Phoenix Trail.
Parking: Car park at start; limited on-street parking near end.
Maps and guides: OS Landranger 165, Explorer 180 & 181.
Website: www.sustrans.org.uk/find-a-route-on-the-national-cycle-network/phoenix-trail-princes-risborough-to-thame

WESTERN COUNTIES

Oxford Canal: Heyford to Oxford
Ride 27

Those seeking to escape the tourist crowds around the college greens are strongly advised to hop on the train with their bikes and head north to Heyford. The canal towpath may sometimes be a bumpy ride, but it offers a tranquil retreat from Oxford's more popular destinations. The narrow, gravel-topped track is best tackled on a gravel or mountain bike.

On your bikes!

1. The trail is easily joined behind Heyford railway station. Turn right on to the trail, keeping the canal to your left. Follow the towpath.

2. Remain on the same side of the towpath, with the canal to your left, ignoring other routes that cross the canal.

3. Continue straight on, following the towpath, ignoring the turnoff to the right at Dukes Lock.

4. The route enters Oxford, passing through Jericho and ending near the Ashmolean Museum.

Refreshments: The Bell Inn, Heyford. Plenty of choice in Oxford.
Bike hire and repairs: Bike hire options in Oxford include Brompton at station, Bainton Bikes, Donkey Bikes and OxonBike docking stations; plenty of bike shops in Oxford.
Public transport and bike links: Heyford station at start. Oxford station 300m from end.
Parking: Very limited on-street parking in Heyford. Paid car parks in Oxford centre. With stations at start and end, this is a great route to tackle by train.
Maps and guides: OS Landranger 164, Explorer 180 & 191.
Website: *canalrivertrust.org.uk/enjoy-the-waterways/cycling/canal-cycling-routes/heyford-to-oxford-cycle-ride*

Start
Heyford railway station, Heyford (51.9186, -1.2993, SP 482246)

Finish
Near the Ashmolean Museum, Oxford (51.7535, -1.2648, SP 508063)

Distance
14.5 miles/23.5km.

Category
Canal towpaths.

Other facilities

77

Greater London

1. Basingstoke Canal: Mytchett Visitor Centre to Byfleet
2. Norbury Park: Leatherhead
3. Wey Navigation: Weybridge to Pyrford Lock
4. Horton Country Park
5. Bushy Park
6. Slough Arm Grand Union Canal, east of Slough
7. Grand Union Canal: north of Denham Country Park
8. Ebury Way: Rickmansworth to West Watford
9. Osterley Park and House
10. Tamsin Trail, Richmond
11. Thames Towpath: Putney Bridge to Weybridge
12. Wandle Trail
13. Hyde Park
14. Greenwich to Erith alongside the Thames
15. Limehouse Basin to Westminster
16. Queen Elizabeth Olympic Park
17. Rainham Marshes
18. Ingrebourne Hill Bike Park
19. Pages Wood
20. Epping Forest
21. Lee Navigation: Waltham Abbey to Islington
22. Lee Navigation: Hertford to Waltham Abbey

Greater London

03

GREATER LONDON

Greater London

79

Ride 1 Basingstoke Canal: Mytchett Visitor Centre to Byfleet

Start
Basingstoke Canal Centre, Mytchett (51.2884, -0.7204, SU 893551)

Finish
Wey Navigation junction, West Byfleet (51.3475, -0.4864, TQ 055620)

Distance
13 miles/21km.

Category
Canal towpaths.

Other facilities

This ride follows the Basingstoke Canal from the visitor centre at Mytchett to the canal's junction with the Wey Navigation near to Byfleet. However, it is not the only stretch of the canal featured in this book – see pages 64 and 65. This ride is predominantly on a wide stone and gravel track through beautiful broadleaf woodland, especially noticeable through the remarkable flight of locks at Deepcut where there are 14 locks in less than two miles. The best-quality towpath on the whole of the canal runs through Woking: wide and smooth with the vegetation cut well back away from the path – a real delight to ride. The end of the canal at its junction with the Wey Navigation is right underneath the M25, and as this is not an especially exciting place you may prefer to continue north up towards Weybridge or south towards Pyrford for refreshments.

Refreshments: Tea room at Canal Centre at Mytchett. Lots of cafes and pubs just off the route through Woking.
Bike hire and repairs: Several bike shops in Woking.
Public transport and bike links: North Camp and Ash Vale stations, 1.5 miles from start. West Byfleet and Byfleet & New Haw rail stations, 1 mile from end.
Parking: Free parking at start. Paid car parks in Byfleet and West Byfleet.
Maps and guides: OS Landranger 186 & 187, Explorer 145 & 160.
Website: basingstoke-canal.org.uk

On your bikes!

1. From the Basingstoke Canal Centre at Mytchett, cross the canal and turn right, keeping the canal to your right.

2. After ³/₄ mile at the B3012 (opposite the King's Head pub), turn right then left to rejoin the canal towpath. The railway line passes under the canal.

3. There may be a 1-mile diversion away from the canal east of the B3015 – follow signs on a track parallel with and to the north of the canal.

4. Rejoin the canal and follow through Brookwood, close to the railway line. The towpath quality improves dramatically at the western edge of Woking.

5. In central Woking you will need to cross Chobham Road using the traffic lights to regain the towpath on the other side.

6. The suggested end point is at the junction with the Wey Navigation beneath the M25. However, you may prefer to follow the Wey Navigation north to Weybridge for 2 miles to find refreshments, or south for 2 miles to the pub at Pyrford Lock (see p82).

GREATER LONDON

Norbury Park Leatherhead

Ride 2

Norbury Park offers a short, waymarked circuit in amongst woodland and farmland, which seems a million miles from the busy roads in this densely populated part of Surrey. There is a good network of bridleways stretching south-east through Polesden Lacey and Ranmore Common along the North Downs towards Shere and Gomshall, so with an Ordnance Survey map you could easily devise your own off-road routes through the woodland. Norbury Park was the first area of countryside that Surrey County Council purchased in the 1930s to protect it from development. Lying within the Surrey Hills Area of Outstanding Natural Beauty and covering 1,300 acres, it comprises an attractive mix of woods, farms and grassland. Much of the park lies on chalk and flint, with a clay cap on higher ground. These soil types support different woodland communities: beech, yew, ash and cherry are classic chalk-area trees, whereas clay supports oak and chestnut. Some of the yews are up to 2,000 years old.

On your bikes!

1. Exit the car park, turn sharp right on the tarmac lane leading directly away from the main road. After around 200m ignore a 'Byway' sign to the right. Continue straight ahead on the main track. Go gently downhill, then at a crossroads with a wooden bench to the right continue straight ahead uphill, gently then more steeply.

2. At a fork of tracks by a wooden barrier and a two-way 'Bridleway' signpost, bear left on the steeper of the two tracks. At the top of the hill at a second fork by a large triangle of grass and trees, with a wooden fence ahead, turn right, going past a timber yard.

3. After ³/₄ mile, at a fork on a tarmac descent not long after passing the viewpoint to the left, bear right on a track climbing to the right, following bike signs.

4. At the T-junction at the end of Crabtree Lane car park, turn right uphill. With a flint and brick house to the left, bear right uphill around a wooden barrier.

5. Long, gentle descent. At a fork bear right alongside woodland. Follow this track past a red-brick farm (Roaring House Farm) then at the next crossroads turn left, signposted 'Fetcham, car park', and follow the outward route back to the start.

Refreshments: The closest are in Leatherhead or Great Bookham.
Bike hire and repairs: Spares and repairs from Surrey Hills Cycleworks, Leatherhead.
Public transport and bike links: Leatherhead station, 1.5 miles from start.
Parking: Free car parking at start.
Maps and guides: OS Landranger 187, Explorer 146.
Website: www.surreywildlifetrust.org/nature-reserves/norbury-park

Start/finish
Norbury Park, near junction of A246 and B2122 (51.2814, -0.3499, TQ 152549)

Distance
4 mile/6.5km circuit.

Category
Good-quality bridleways.

Other facilities

81

Ride 3 Wey Navigation: Weybridge to Pyrford Lock

Start
The Old Crown pub, Weybridge (51.3791, -0.4556, TQ 076656)

Finish
Pyrford Marina, Woking (51.3227, -0.4901, TQ 053593)

Distance
5 miles/8km.

Category
Canal towpaths.

Other facilities

NB The Wey Navigation towpath can also be followed for 5 miles at its southern end between Guildford and Godalming.

There are several traffic-free options for escaping from south-west London along the waterways: the Thames Towpath runs from Putney Bridge to Weybridge (p91) and the Basingstoke Canal starts south of Weybridge and runs south-west through Woking to Odiham in Hampshire (p80). Connecting the two and taking a more southerly course, the Wey Navigation starts in Weybridge and heads through Byfleet towards Guildford and Godalming. South of Pyrford to Guildford, the canal towpath is fairly rough, but the five-mile stretch described here is in reasonable condition and offers a chance to enjoy a ride along a green corridor through this built-up area, ending at a waterside pub at Pyrford Lock.

On your bikes!

1. By the side of the Old Crown pub turn down Church Walk. Walk for 50m.

2. At the end of the path turn right, cross the ornate metal bridge then at the T-junction turn left, signposted 'Flockton House', and shortly turn right on to a wide gravel path alongside green railings. Dismount to cross a humpback metal bridge and turn left on the towpath.

3. At times narrow and rooty. After ³/₄ mile, at a grey-brick bridge at the T-junction with Addlestone Road, turn right, signposted 'Addlestone/Chertsey Bike Route'. You may prefer to ride on the road parallel to the canal as a more comfortable option for ¹/₄ mile as far as the humpback bridge on your left, where the towpath changes sides.

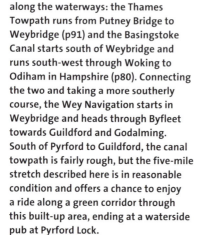

GREATER LONDON

Wey Navigation: Weybridge to Pyrford Lock Ride 3

4. You will occasionally need to cross roads as the towpath changes sides. Pass beneath the M25* following signs for Guildford and Godalming. It is suggested you continue for 2 miles beyond the canal junction as far as the Anchor pub at Pyrford Marina, then return to Weybridge. About 1 mile beyond Pyrford Marina the towpath becomes much rougher.

*At the point where you pass under the M25 you have the option of turning right off the Wey Navigation and following the Basingstoke Canal for many miles through Woking, Aldershot and Fleet to Odiham.

Refreshments: Lots of choice in Weybridge: The Minnow pub; Old Crown pub at the start. The Anchor at Pyrford Lock.
Bike hire and repairs: Zabikes Pro Cycle Repair, in Shepperton across river from start, can be reached by ferry.
Public transport and bike links: Weybridge station, 1.5 miles from start; Addlestone rail station 1 mile from Town Lock, Weybridge. West Byfleet station, 2 miles from end. Route connects with several other routes: Thames Towpath can be followed to Putney Bridge, also crosses Basingstoke Canal at West Byfleet.
Parking: Free car park at Weybridge Point, larger car park further along river at Walton Bridge; no parking at end except in Pyrford town centre.
Maps and guides: OS Landranger 176 & 187, Explorer 145 & 160.

83

Ride 4 Horton Country Park

Start/finish
Horton Country Park, north-west of Epsom
(51.3432, -0.2916, TQ 191618)

Distance
3 miles/5km.

Category
Cycle paths.

Other facilities

This short circuit around Horton Country Park takes you past a mixture of woodland, farmland and through a golf course – as you are not crossing any greens you should be safe from flying golf balls! Part of the route uses the course of the old Horton Light Railway, a branch line that was used to supply coal to the hospital boiler house. In springtime some of the woods are covered with a carpet of bluebells, indicating that the woodlands have grown undisturbed for many years. There is also a circuit around Epsom Common starting from the car park, located on the south side of the B280 (Christ Church Road), about two miles to the west of Epsom.

Refreshments: Cafe at the Old Moat Garden Centre next to park. Lots of choice in Epsom.
Bike hire and repairs: Several bike shops in Epsom.
Public transport and bike links: Chessington North and Chessington South stations within a mile north of park.
Parking: Free car parking at start.
Maps and guides: OS Landranger 187, Explorer 161.
Website: www.visitsurrey.com/things-to-do/horton-country-park-p1257011

On your bikes!
1. Exit the car park and turn right. At major track crossroads go straight ahead, signposted 'Horseride, Chessington Countryside Walk' (the track to the left is the return route). Ignore a left turn. Shortly at a fork of tracks with low wooden posts to the right, bear right.

2. Gentle descent. At the T-junction by large concrete slabs, turn right. Go past a pond and between golf greens. At the crossroads of tracks at the top of a short rise, turn left. Bear right at a series of forks.

3. At the track T-junction with a narrow grass track ahead, turn left. At the crossroads of tracks by a red-tile-hung house, turn right to return to the start.

84

GREATER LONDON

Bushy Park Ride 5

There are eight royal parks in London, owned by the Crown, and Bushy Park is the second largest (nearby neighbour Richmond is bigger). It is next to Hampton Court Palace, and although its days of being used as a royal hunting ground are in the past, it is still home to herds of deer. There are miles of pretty parkland paths, as well as the seventeenth-century Diana Fountain, to enjoy. There are short sections of road to negotiate (at Kingston Bridge, for example, and by Hampton Court Palace); you may prefer to dismount and use the pavement for these short sections.

On your bikes!

1. From the Diana Fountain, follow the tarmac path south through the Royal Paddocks to the Church Grove gate. Turn right on to Hampton Court Road, and then right towards Kingston Bridge; do not cross the river but turn right just before the bridge on to Barge Walk.

2. Follow the Thames Path along the river, past Hampton Court Palace Golf Club and Hampton Court Palace.

3. Turn right on to Hampton Court Road, follow it past Hampton Court Palace and shortly after it bends right, turn left on Chestnut Avenue to re-enter Bushy Park; you will encounter traffic on this stretch of park road. Just before the Diana Fountain, turn left on the Hampton Wick path. At the path T-junction, turn left and after 600m, turn right.

4. After 200m, fork left. After another 200m, fork left again and after 300m, turn right at the T-junction. After 450m, at the crossroads turn right on to Cobbler's Walk. After 1/2 mile, turn left.

Follow the track around the perimeter of the park until you reach the path past the Royal Paddocks; turn right to return to the start.

Refreshments: Pheasantry Cafe, near visitor centre.
Bike hire and repairs: Spares and repairs from Burts Cycles, Moore's Cycles or Birdie Bikes. Brompton Bike Hire at Surbiton station.
Public transport and bike links: Hampton Court and Hampton Wick rail stations within 500m of park gates. National Cycle Network (NCN) Route 4 offers a route from Bushy Park into central London.
Parking: Four free car parks in Bushy Park.
Maps and guides: OS Landranger 176 & Explorer 161; a London street map may be more useful.
Website: www.royalparks.org.uk/parks/bushy-park

Start/finish
Diana Fountain, Bushy Park
(51.4112, -0.3340, TQ 158691)

Distance
8.5 miles/13.5km.

Category
Gravel and tarmac cycle paths, park roads, roads.

Other facilities

© YONI DITAL

Ride 6 Slough Arm Grand Union Canal east of Slough

Start
Cowley Peachey Junction, 3 miles south of Uxbridge (51.5202, -0.4828, TQ 054812)

Finish
B416 Stoke Road, north of Slough railway station (51.5173, -0.5897, SU 979808)

Distance
5.5 miles/9km.

Category
Canal towpaths.

Other facilities

There are several 'arms' coming off the Grand Union Canal north-west of London: in addition to the one described here, others are to be found at Wendover, Aylesbury and Northampton. The Slough Arm runs from Slough via Langley and Iver to the Cowley Peachey Junction (south of Uxbridge). Built in 1882, the Slough Arm was, with the exception of the Manchester Ship Canal and New Junction Canal, the last canal to be built in Britain. It goes over several aqueducts and through a long cutting. To the west of Iver the water is surprisingly clear.

On your bikes!
1. Access the canal from Packet Boat Lane. Follow the towpath for 400m and turn right to join the Slough Arm.
2. Follow the towpath along the Slough Arm for 5 miles to its terminus near Slough.

Refreshments: The WatersEdge pub at start; options in Iver, Langley and Slough near canal.
Bike hire and repairs: Several bike shops in Slough, including Bike Shed, 200m from end of Slough Arm.
Public transport and bike links: West Drayton station, 1/2 mile from start of Slough Arm; Slough station, 1/2 mile from end. National Cycle Network (NCN) Route 61 (on- and off-road) provides an alternative route between Slough and Cowley.
Parking: On-road parking near start. Paid car parks near Slough station.
Maps and guides: OS Landranger 176, Explorer 160 & 172.
Website: *canalrivertrust.org.uk/ enjoy-the-waterways/canal-and-river-network/slough-arm-grand-union-canal*

86

GREATER LONDON

Grand Union Canal: Ride 7
north of Denham Country Park

With the exception of a five-mile section in London between Kensal Rise and Horsenden Hill (near Wembley), very little of the Grand Union Canal from Paddington right through to Uxbridge offers good recreational cycling: the towpath is too narrow, too rough, too overgrown or very slow, with a succession of metal anti-motorbike barriers. To the north of Uxbridge things start to improve, and Denham Country Park is a good starting point for exploration further north. Having said this, mountain bikes or gravel bikes are definitely recommended as there are still some short, rougher sections. The towpath is a green corridor past hundreds of brightly coloured narrowboats. The Batchworth Canal Centre or the cafe at Rickmansworth Aquadrome are good destinations, although you have two options for extending your trip: along the Ebury Way (a railway path) into Watford (next ride), or on a continuation of the towpath to the west of Watford, towards Hemel Hempstead.

On your bikes!

1. From the Colne Valley Park Visitor Centre in Denham Country Park go back under the height barrier, turn left then right through the overflow car park, bearing left through the car park itself to pick up 'Grand Union Canal' signs. Follow the gravel path to the canal and turn left. **Remember** this point for your return (near Bridge 182).

2. Go past the tea gardens at the lock. About $1/2$ mile after Bridge 180 and the River Garden pub there is a rougher and narrower section to Bridge 179.

3. Go past the Coy Carp pub and Copper Mill Lock. The path is again a bit rougher either side of a concrete bridge with raised humps across it.

4. After 2 miles you will come to Batchworth Canal Centre, just beyond Rickmansworth Aquadrome. It is suggested you turn around here after visiting the centre and/or the cafe at the Aquadrome.

5. If you wish to extend your ride you can either stay on the Grand Union Canal towpath on its way towards Kings Langley and Hemel Hempstead, or follow the Ebury Way along the course of an old railway line into Watford.

Refreshments: Cafe at Denham Country Park Visitor Centre; River Garden pub; South Harefield; Coy Carp pub Coppermill Lane. Cafe at the Aquadrome.
Bike hire and repairs: Bikewise shop, Ickenham, 3 miles from start.
Public transport and bike links: Rickmansworth station, 1 mile from end or Denham station, $2/3$ mile from canal near start.
Parking: Free parking at Rickmansworth Aquadrome. Paid parking at Denham Country Park.
Maps and guides: OS Landranger 176, Explorer 172.
Website: *canalrivertrust.org.uk/enjoy-the-waterways/canal-and-river-network/grand-union-canal*

Start
Visitor Centre, Denham Country Park (51.5671, -0.4896, TQ 048864)

Finish
Rickmansworth Aquadrome, Rickmansworth (51.6333, -0.4733, TQ 058938)

Distance
6 miles/10km.

Category
Canal towpaths.

Other facilities

87

Ride 8 Ebury Way: Rickmansworth to West Watford

Start
Rickmansworth Aquadrome, Rickmansworth (51.6333, -0.4733, TQ 058918)

Finish
A4178 Wiggenhall Road, Watford (51.6463, -0.3952, TQ 111954)

Distance
4 miles/6km.

Category
Canal towpaths, railway paths.

Other facilities

This four-mile railway path between Rickmansworth and West Watford is surprisingly green and leafy for such a built-up area. The trail crosses the Colne, Chess and Gade rivers and if you are lucky you may even see the flash of bright blue as a kingfisher flies low over the water. The path runs parallel with, then crosses, the Grand Union Canal, so it would be easy to vary the there-and-back ride along the railway by returning via the canal towpath. Indeed, the Grand Union Canal could be followed for several miles in either direction, either south towards Uxbridge or north towards Hemel Hempstead and Berkhamsted. As the year progresses the dominant features of the ride change from birdsong in spring to wildflowers and dragonflies in the summer, then berries on blackthorn, hawthorn and bramble in the autumn, offering important food sources for the resident thrushes and blackbirds but also migrants such as redwings and fieldfares.

Refreshments: Cafe at Rickmansworth Aquadrome at the start of the ride. Plenty of choice in Watford.
Bike hire and repairs: Beryl (docking) Bikes in Watford; docking station at Riverside Park, at end of ride. Watford Cycle Hub for hire, spares and repairs, several bike shops in Watford.
Public transport and bike links: Riverside Park served by hourly buses between Watford and South Oxhey. Bushey rail and underground station, $1/2$ mile from end. Rickmansworth station, 1 mile from start. Trail is part of National Cycle Network (NCN) 6 (London to Threlkeld) and NCN 61 (Maidenhead to Hoddesdon) cycle routes.
Parking: Free parking at Aquadrome. Paid parking at Oxhey Activity Park, adjacent to end.
Maps and guides: OS Landranger 176, Explorer 172 & 173.

On your bikes!

1. With the canal in front of you, turn left on to the canal towpath. Pass beneath the main road then immediately after the Batchworth Canal Centre bear left, cross a wooden bridge to the left and follow the path.

2. With a low 'drawbridge' to the right, turn left then shortly turn sharp right through metal posts/barriers and a car park to join the Ebury Way.

3. The Ebury Way, signposted as 'National Cycle Network Route 6', ends after 3 miles at the A4178 Wiggenhall Road, south of Watford.

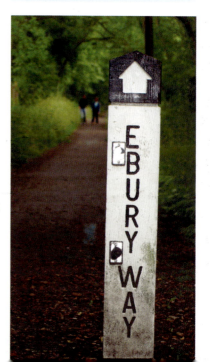

GREATER LONDON

Osterley Park and House — Ride 9

Osterley Park is a National Trust estate in west London. The Georgian estate is home to an eighteenth-century, red-brick, turreted house, formal gardens and acres of parkland to explore. In addition to the house, there is a cafe and a second-hand bookshop. In 2017, the National Trust constructed a 1.5-mile, shared-use track around the perimeter of the grounds for walkers and cyclists to enjoy. In addition to cycle hire, cycle lessons are also available at Osterley Park and there is a cycle skills area. This is the perfect site for a novice or child rider to gain confidence in a safe environment.

Refreshments: National Trust cafe near start.
Bike hire and repairs: Cycle hire on Front Lawn, Osterley Park. Bike shops in Hounslow.
Public transport and bike links: Syon Lane station, 1 mile from park; Osterley underground on park perimeter.
Parking: Paid National Trust parking near start.
Maps and guides: OS Landranger 176, Explorer 161; a London street map may be more useful.
Website: *www.nationaltrust.org.uk/osterley-park-and-house*

Start/finish
Osterley House, Isleworth
(51.4895, -0.3517, TQ 145780)

Distance
1.5 miles/2.5km.

Category
Multi-use tracks.

Other facilities

On your bikes!

1. With Osterley House behind you, turn right and follow the trail around the lake.

2. Turn left along the edge of the car park and past the cycling skills area.

3. Bear right at the fork. Turn left on to Osterley Lane; there is a chicane barrier to negotiate here.

4. Follow the trail around Middle Lake, remaining on Osterley Lane. Turn left on to Elm Drive to return to the house.

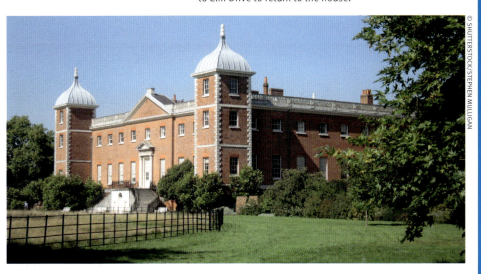
© SHUTTERSTOCK/STEPHEN MULLIGAN

TRAFFIC-FREE CYCLE TRAILS SOUTH EAST ENGLAND

Ride 10 Tamsin Trail Richmond

Start/finish
Roehampton Gate, Richmond Park
(51.4538, -0.2572, TQ 212742)

Distance
8 miles/13km.

Category
Cycle tracks.

Other facilities

NB Several roads are crossed in the park, so take care if you are with young children.

Created by the generosity of an anonymous donor who wanted the trail named after his daughter, Tamsin, this eight-mile, purpose-built circuit of Richmond Park is one of the best things to have happened to recreational cycling in London. The trail runs along a fine gravel path with several gentle hills. The park lies on the sloping plateau above Richmond. It was enclosed by Charles I in 1637 with an eight-mile wall, enabling him to hunt for deer. From Pembroke Lodge, on the western edge of the park, the views on a clear day extend far into Berkshire. To the north of Pembroke Lodge is King Henry VIII's mound where it is possible to see the dome of St Paul's Cathedral.

On your bikes!

1. You can start anywhere on this circular route, but Roehampton Gate is a good choice because there is food, toilets and Parkcycle near the gate. The trail, which circumnavigates the perimeter of the park, is well marked. The route is easier if tackled anticlockwise.

Refreshments: Cafe at Pembroke Lodge on the west side of the park; Roehampton Gate cafe at start.
Bike hire and repairs: Bike hire from Parkcycle (in park); Richmond Station Cycle Centre; Blazing Saddles Bike Hire. Several bike shops in Richmond and Twickenham.
Public transport and bike links: Kingston, Richmond, North Sheen and Mortlake stations all approximately 1 mile from park. Thames Towpath runs through Richmond and National Cycle Network (NCN) Route 4 offers (on- and off-road) route into central London.
Parking: Free car parks near park gate entrances.
Maps and guides: OS Landranger 176, Explorer 161.
Website: www.royalparks.org.uk/parks/richmond-park

90

GREATER LONDON

Thames Towpath: Putney Bridge to Weybridge
Ride 11

The Thames Towpath is the best exit from the city for cyclists from south-west London, with plenty to see along this wonderful green and leafy corridor, including Hampton Court Palace. There is a striking contrast between the wide, untamed tidal stretch as far west as Teddington Lock and the highly managed pleasure boat section which lies beyond. The towpath overlaps entirely with National Cycle Network (NCN) Route 4 for the second half of the ride for 11 miles, from Teddington Lock through Kingston to Weybridge, and it is here that the quality of the towpath is at its very best. For the section between Putney Bridge and Teddington (a section where NCN 4 takes an alternative route across Richmond Park), the quality is variable and mountain or gravel bikes are recommended. There is one quite rough patch between Hammersmith Bridge and Chiswick Bridge.

On your bikes!
1. There is a short section between Hammersmith Bridge and Barnes railway bridge (along Lonsdale Road), where there is no towpath. It is suggested you walk along the pavement for about 550m. The towpath is very narrow, close to Chiswick Bridge.

2. In Kingston you should follow 'National Cycle Network 4' signs, turning left away from the river at a grey metal 'Meccano' bridge in the direction of 'Kingston Town Centre'. There is a safe, waymarked route through the traffic on green-painted cycle lanes signposted 'NCN 4' that will take you across Kingston Bridge.

3. After Hampton Court station, cross the road at the toucan crossing, turn left across the bridge and then right at the end of the bridge to continue alongside the river towards Walton-on-Thames.

4. The canal towpath is straightforward to follow for another 16.5 miles, all the way to Weybridge.

Refreshments: All along the way.
Bike hire and repairs: Santander Cycles docking station, Putney Bridge; Blazing Saddles Bike Hire, en route at Richmond. Spares and repairs from Elswood Cycleworks and Barnes Bikes near start. Plenty of cycle shops in Twickenham and Richmond.
Public transport and bike links: Putney station, 500m from start. Richmond station, 2 miles from end; Twickenham station, 1.5 miles (via ferry) from end. Lots of underground stations close to route. NCN 4 continues on into central London, and to Fishguard in Wales.
Parking: Paid car parks in Wandsworth. Small riverside car park on the sharp bend on Thames Street/Walton Lane at end. Route falls within ULEZ.
Maps and guides: OS Landranger 176, Explorer 161; a London street map may be more useful.
Website: www.nationaltrail.co.uk/en_GB/trails/thames-path

Start
Putney Bridge, Putney (51.4665, -0.2153, TQ 240757)

Finish
Weybridge landing, Weybridge (51.3817, -0.4564, TQ 075 658)

Distance
Up to 23 miles/ 37km.

Category
Riverside paths.

Other facilities

NB Please note that the towpath is frequently busy with pedestrians, particularly on summer weekends, so please slow down and show consideration.

91

Ride 12 Wandle Trail

Start
Deen City Farm, Merton (51.4086, -0.1844, TQ 264693)

Finish
Carshalton Water Tower, Carshalton (51.3650, -0.1666, TQ 277645)

Distance
4.5 miles/7.5km.

Category
Riverside paths, tarmac trails.

Other facilities

The Wandle Trail follows the River Wandle from its junction with the River Thames to East Croydon. The 12.5-mile trail takes advantage of riverside paths, parks and green spaces, and the occasional road section. Through the start section you will find yourself forced back on to the road, so this describes the route from Morden to Carshalton. There are some road crossings to negotiate, some with narrow paths and barriers.

On your bikes!

1. Starting by the Deen City Farm, follow the riverside trail as it meanders through the National Trust's Morden Hall Park.

2. Turn right on Morden Road for 150m. Cross the road and turn left on to a trail by the river that emerges into Ravensbury Park.

3. Cross London Road and continue straight ahead, along the trail; there are bollards on the entrance. The trail takes you through the Watermead Wetlands.

4. The trail emerges via the no through road Watermead Lane (**be wary** of cars parking) – use the pedestrian crossing to the right to cross the road. The trail continues straight ahead.

5. Continue on the riverside trail, crossing the River Wandle near Watercress Park. Cross Culvers Avenue (there are chicane barriers) and continue straight ahead.

6. At Hackbridge Road, turn right on the road for 50m before crossing the river. Return to the river trail next to the park. The trail now passes through the Wilderness Island Nature Reserve to finish near Carshalton Ponds and the water tower.

Refreshments: Plenty of choice close to the route, including cafe at Deen City Farm and several options in Carshalton.

Bike hire and repairs: Spares and repairs from Village Bike Shop in Carshalton.

Public transport and bike links: South Merton station, 1 mile from start. Carshalton rail station, 500m from end.

Parking: On-street parking near start. The Square (paid) car park adjacent to end. Route within ULEZ.

Maps and guides: OS Landranger 176, Explorer 161; a London street map may be more useful.

Website: *www.sustrans.org.uk/find-a-route-on-the-national-cycle-network/wandle-trail*

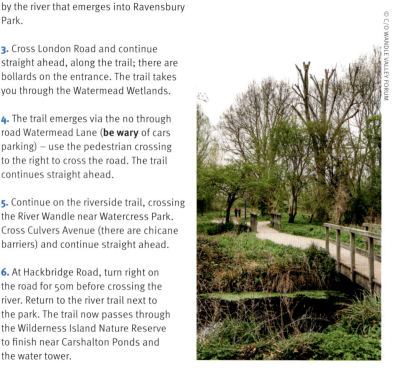

© C/O WANDLE VALLEY FORUM

GREATER LONDON

Hyde Park Ride 13

Hyde Park is perhaps London's most famous green space, in the heart of Central London. With astonishing works of art dotted around the parkland, the artificial Serpentine Lake and the famous Speakers' Corner, there is plenty to explore by bicycle. The park is a popular venue for events, from the London Half Marathon to the annual Winter Wonderland, so check what's going on in the park before you visit.

On your bikes!

1. From Hyde Park Corner, turn left to follow the segregated cycle path beside South Carriage Drive. **Take care** when crossing Exhibition Road, and continue straight ahead, following the cycle path into the park.

2. Turn right on to Broad Walk. Turn right at the end of Broad Walk and follow the cycle path along the North Carriage Drive.

3. Near Cumberland Gate, turn right to follow the cycle path around the perimeter of the park to return to the start.

Refreshments: Bar, cafes and kiosks within the park.
Bike hire and repairs: Several Santander Cycles docking stations in and on edge of park; one at start. Fettle bike repair, Connaught Village and LEZ Cycles, Queensway.
Public transport and bike links: Lancaster Gate, Queensway, Marble Arch, Hyde Park Corner and Knightsbridge underground stations on perimeter of park; Paddington rail station 500m from park.
Parking: Limited paid parking within Hyde Park; private car parks on perimeter of park. Hyde Park within Congestion Charge and ULEZ.
Maps and guides: OS Landranger 176, Explorer 173; a London street map may be more useful.
Website: www.royalparks.org.uk/parks/hyde-park

Start/finish
Hyde Park Corner, Knightsbridge
(51.5035, -0.1526, TQ 283799)

Distance
4 miles/6.5km.

Category
Tarmac cycle paths.

Other facilities

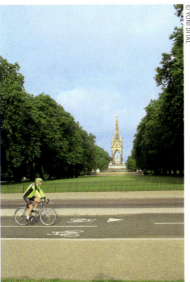

93

Ride 14 Greenwich to Erith alongside the Thames

Start
By the Cutty Sark, Greenwich (51.4824, -0.0099, TQ 383178)

Finish
Erith rail station, Bexley (51.4817, 0.1758, TQ 512191)

Distance
13 miles/21km.

Category
Riverside paths.

Other facilities

Earlier in the book, Ride 11 (p91) explores the River Thames as it enters London from the west; this ride shows a very different face of the river as it approaches the final part of its journey to the sea. Starting in Greenwich, site of the Cutty Sark and the splendour of the Royal Naval College, the ride initially weaves its way through streets to emerge beneath the O2 Arena. The silver shell structures of the Thames Barrier offer a memorable landmark. Beyond here there is a short, unavoidable section on-road before rejoining the river near the Woolwich Ferry. East of here the character of the river is dominated by the shipping of sand and gravel. It is a wide commercial waterway, far removed from the pleasure boats and wooded banks of the River Thames to the west of the city. There is plenty to see along the way, from metal sculptures to old wooden wharfs. The trail improves as it goes further east, becoming a wide, smooth path leading to Erith where you have several options (see step 4).

On your bikes!

1. The route between Greenwich and the O2 Arena does not lie right by the river, so you will need to follow 'Thames Cycle Route/National Cycle Network Route 1' signs closely.

2. Pass around the peninsula beneath the outside of the O2 Arena.

3. Follow close to the river as far as the distinctive silver structures of the Thames Barrier. At this point, you will once again need to leave the river on a well-signposted route along residential streets (and on a cycle path alongside the busier Woolwich Road) to return to the river close to the Woolwich Ferry.

Refreshments: Lots of choice in Greenwich, Woolwich and Erith.
Bike hire and repairs: Greenwich Cycle Hire at the Flight Centre; Greenwich Cycle Workshop for spares and repairs. No Santander Cycles docks – closest are across river in Docklands.
Public transport and bike links: Greenwich station, 400m from start. Erith rail station, at end. Other stations close to route; nearest tube station is North Greenwich, 2.5 miles from start. Greenwich is at a crossroads of the National Cycle Network (NCN) – the best nearby traffic-free section runs north from Limehouse Basin along the Regent's Canal (Grand Union Canal) and through Victoria Park to the Lee Navigation; NCN 4 runs into Central London. Bikes are allowed on the cable car across River Thames; cyclists travel for free before 9.30 a.m. Monday–Friday.
Parking: Paid parking in Greenwich, within ULEZ. Limited options in Erith.
Maps and guides: OS Landranger 177, Explorer 162; a London street map may be more useful.
Website: www.sustrans.org.uk/find-other-routes/thamesmead-to-greenwich

4. A 6-mile riverside section follows all the way to Erith. Here you may wish to turn round, catch a train back to Greenwich or carry on along National Cycle Network (NCN) Route 1 on the banks of the River Darent and River Cray into Dartford.

GREATER LONDON

Limehouse Basin to Westminster   Ride 15

Cycle Superhighway 3 was one of 12 'motorways of cycling' proposed by Ken Livingstone in 2008, and opened in 2010. It runs parallel to the River Thames through the East End borough of Tower Hamlets. Passing the Battle of Cable Street mural, the Tower of London, Big Ben and the Houses of Parliament, it is the perfect London sightseeing tour by bicycle. Although often running alongside busy roads, the cycleway is completely segregated except for a 100-metre section that is shared with buses by the Tower of London, and another short section at Blackfriars which shares access (not through) routes for vehicles. Cycle Superhighway 3 extends eastwards to Barking, but much of it past Limehouse is on-road.

On your bikes!
1. Follow the blue cycleway over the bridge and through St James' Gardens, then cross Butcher Row using the toucan crossing and turn into Cable Street. Follow the blue cycleway along Cable Street (look out for the mural on the side of Shadwell Station) and on into Royal Mint Street.

2. The crossing of the Inner Ring Road is light controlled, but you might prefer to dismount and use the neighbouring pelican crossing to reach Shorter Street (shared with buses). Pass the Tower of London on the segregated path and continue on towards Blackfriars, where the route near Blackfriars Bridge has short sections on access roads.

3. The route finishes with a riverside stretch along the popular Victoria Embankment cycleway, passing HQS Wellington and Cleopatra's Needle to reach Big Ben and the front of the Houses of Parliament (you can continue on a little further to reach Ride 13 (p93) around Hyde Park).

Refreshments: Lots of choice en route, particularly at Limehouse, Tower Hill and Blackfriars.
Bike hire and repairs: Limehouse Bicycle Company (300m from start, on route) for spares and repairs. Santander Cycles docking station under the railway bridge, Flamborough Street, 250m from Horseferry Road and at Westminster Pier, 50m from the Houses of Parliament (on route).
Public transport and bike links: Limehouse station and DLR 300m from start. Westminster underground at end; Charing Cross rail station $1/2$ mile from end.
Parking: Parking near Shadwell Basin and St Katharine Docks, and at Westminster and Waterloo; congestion and ULEZ charges may also apply.
Maps and guides: OS Landranger 177 & 176, Explorer 173; a London street map may be more useful.
Website: *tfl.gov.uk/modes/cycling/routes-and-maps/cycleways*

Start
Horseferry Road, Limehouse
(51.5107, -0.0395, TQ 361809)

Finish
Houses of Parliament, Westminster
(51.5008, -0.1241, TQ 303797)

Distance
4 miles/7km.

Category
Blue segregated cycleways.

Other facilities

© LEE VALLEY REGIONAL PARK AUTHORITY

95

Ride 16   Queen Elizabeth Olympic Park

Start/finish
VeloPark, Queen Elizabeth Olympic Park (51.5493, -0.0161, TQ 377852)

Distance
4 miles/6.5km.

Category
Gravel and tarmac cycle paths.

Other facilities

The Queen Elizabeth Olympic Park, on the edge of Hackney Marshes, was built to accommodate the 2012 London Olympics. It retains many of its world-class sporting facilities, but now the general public can visit for a swim, game of tennis or bouldering session. This ride starts at the iconic VeloPark (where you can try your hand at track racing, mountain biking or BMXing) and explores the parkland, rivers and canals while passing many of the famous Olympic venues. There are plenty of other trails to explore in the park, as well as routes north of the park around Hackney Marshes and the Lee Valley.

On your bikes!

1. With the VeloPark behind you, cycle away on the track that takes you beside the Olympic Rings, rather than in front of them. After 250m, by the Timber Lodge, turn right.

2. Follow the trail as it curves around the Blossom Garden, up to the Olympic Rings and around the sharp bend. Around 250m after the bend, take the right-hand fork towards the river.

3. About 50m after crossing under two bridges, fork left and left again. At a track crossroads, turn right to loop the wetlands. Follow the path back round towards the river and cross the Eastcross Bridge, then turn left on to Middlesex Way.

4. Continue straight on, using the segregated cycle lane on Marshgate Road. Turn sharp left along the riverbank. Turn right, crossing the river after 250m, with the Orbit sculpture ahead of you.

5. Follow the trail down the island, passing to the left of the Orbit sculpture. Cross the river on the blue bridge and turn left. Cross the river at Carpenters Road and return to Eastcross Bridge via Marshgate Lane and Middlesex Way.

6. Do not cross the river: take the right fork to follow a trail by the river. Follow it to the north end of the park, and then as it bends around Hopkins Field. After a kinked section of track, turn right to reach Knights Bridge. Cross the river here to return to the start.

Refreshments: The Last Drop and Timber Lodge cafes, and kiosks on Tessa Jowell Boulevard, all en route.
Bike hire and repairs: Several Santander Cycles docks in park, including one at VeloPark. Spares and repairs from Wicked Bike Repair, Frankenbike and About the Bike East in Hackney Wick.
Public transport and bike links: Stratford International rail station and Hackney Wick underground, 200m from park. National Cycle Network (NCN) Route 1 passes through park.
Parking: No general car parking (for venue users only); paid on-street parking and car parks in Stratford. Within ULEZ.
Maps and guides: OS Landranger 177, Explorer 162 & 174; a London street map may be more useful.
Website: www.queenelizabetholympicpark.co.uk

GREATER LONDON

Rainham Marshes   Ride 17

This Royal Society for the Protection of Birds (RSPB) Nature Reserve is the perfect place for a family outing. This flat, circular loop (the RSPB's Reserve Loop – see website) offers fantastic views of the Thames, a chance to wonder at the World War II concrete barges and plenty of opportunity for bird spotting. It is hard to believe that this wetland area has been transformed, since 2000, from a military firing range. There is also a visitor centre, cafe and toilets. There is an almost entirely traffic-free route between Purfleet and Rainham railway stations which runs through the reserve; this route connects with National Cycle Network (NCN) 13 which offers an on- and off-road route into central London. There is a frame barrier on the route, and one road crossing.

On your bikes!

1. With the visitor centre behind you, turn right to follow the NCN-waymarked park along the banks of the River Thames. At a T-junction after a mile, take the left fork to remain beside the river.

2. After 1.5 miles, near the concrete barges, the trail begins to wiggle inland.

3. Just before the trail meets Coldharbour Lane, turn right; the route to Rainham station continues straight on here. After $1/2$ mile, cross Coldharbour Lane to remain on the trail.

4. After $2/3$ mile, you reach the T-junction near the visitor centre (step 1); turn left to return to the start.

Refreshments: Cafe at start.
Bike hire and repairs: Bike hire at start.
Public transport and bike links: Purfleet station 1 mile from start; traffic-free route from Purfleet to Rainham rail stations runs through reserve. NCN 13 offers link into central London.
Parking: Free parking at start (donation suggested); entrance charge for reserve, except for local residents.
Maps and guides: OS Landranger 177, Explorer 162.
Website: *www.rspb.org.uk/reserves-and-events/reserves-a-z/rainham-marshes*

Start/finish
Rainham Marshes Visitor Centre, Purfleet (51.4866, 0.2275, TQ 548788)

Distance
5 miles/8.5km.

Category
Hard-surfaced trails.

Other facilities

© ROBIN STEPHENSON/NEWHAM CYCLISTS

Ride 18 Ingrebourne Hill Bike Park

Start/finish
Ingrebourne Hill Bike Park general trail (51.5262, 0.1939, TQ 523831) or mountain bike trail, Rainham (51.5303, 0.1977, TQ 525836)

Distance
2 miles/3.5km or 1.5 miles/2.5km.

Category
Hard-surfaced cycle paths, mountain bike trails.

Other facilities

If the tarmac trails of nearby Rainham Marshes (previous ride) don't get you in the saddle, perhaps you'll prefer the mountain bike tracks on Forestry England's Ingrebourne Hill. There's a 2-mile route, and a 1.5-mile mountain bike track. Trails also run through the forest which link Ingrebourne Hill with Rainham Marshes. There are lakeside picnic spots, and plenty of opportunity for wildlife watching in this urban escape.

On your bikes!

1. The general cycle trail follows the perimeter of the park; you can extend the 2-mile route by venturing into Hornchurch Country Park or following the Ingrebourne Valley trail.

2. There is a 1.5 mile/2km mountain bike route around the centre of the park.

Refreshments: Albion pub near start.
Bike hire and repairs: Bike hire at nearby Rainham Marshes; bike shops in Dagenham.
Public transport and bike links: Rainham station, $^1/_2$ mile from park. Ingrebourne Valley trail links to Rainham Marshes.
Parking: Free parking at start.
Maps and guides: OS Landranger 177, Explorer 162.
Website: www.forestryengland.uk/ingrebourne-hill

© FORESTRY ENGLAND

GREATER LONDON

Pages Wood Ride 19

The Thames Chase is a community forest, one of 12 in England, which is spread across 47 sites in London and Essex. Over the last 30 years, more than 3 million trees have been planted to create new woodland havens in urban areas. Pages Wood in Havering is the largest Forestry England site in the Thames Chase, and offers four miles of family friendly, traffic-free cycle paths. The suggested route loops through the forest, but there are miles of cycle paths in the woods to explore.

On your bikes!

1. At the path junction, near the car park, take the minor trail north, past the dog waste bin. At the path T-junction in 400m, turn right.

2. After another 400m, turn right at the T-junction, and shortly after right again. After $^1/_2$ mile, fork left to reach the northernmost edge of the woods. After 550m, at a track crossroads, turn right.

3. After $^1/_2$ mile, turn right to return to the track crossroads and turn right. Remain on this track for 450m, ignoring the track to the left.

4. At the T-junction, turn left and at a second T-junction, left again. After 60m, turn right (on to the track in step 2) and follow this trail back to the car park.

Refreshments: Pubs and cafes in Harold Wood.
Bike hire and repairs: Halfords Romford, 1.5 miles north of woods.
Public transport and bike links: Harold Wood station, $^1/_2$ mile from northern edge of Pages Wood. National Cycle Network (NCN) 136/the Ingrebourne Valley trail runs through Pages Wood.
Parking: Free car parking at start.
Maps and guides: OS Landranger 177, Explorer 175.
Website: *forestryengland.uk/pages-wood*

Start/finish
Hall Lane Road car park, Pages Wood (51.5814, 0.2524, TQ 562894)

Distance
3 miles/4.5km.

Category
Forestry trails, some rough surfaced.

Other facilities

© TAMARA STOLL

Ride 20 Epping Forest

Start/finish
Kings Oak pub, High Beach
(51.6643, 0.0400, TQ 412981)

Distance
8 miles/5km (although there are many miles of track from which to make up your own routes).

Category
Forest trails.

Other facilities

NB Great care should be taken crossing the roads, particularly the A104 and A121 which are both crossed twice. Allow yourself time to gauge the speed of the traffic and wait for a clear gap in both directions.

There is such a plethora of top-grade gravel tracks in Epping Forest that it would be possible to make up any number of routes criss-crossing this ancient woodland, which is owned and managed by the Corporation of London. This ride starts from the Kings Oak pub in the heart of the forest and wastes no time before diving into the wooded delights on a broad gravel track. There are some roads to be crossed during the course of the ride and great care should be taken on the crossings of the busier ones. As long as you are prepared to wait for a clear gap in the traffic, the roads should not be a deterrent to exploring Epping Forest's fine network of tracks. It is notoriously difficult to give woodland instructions so please do not get exasperated if you feel you are lost! The most important point is that you are outside cycling in beautiful woodland, you will never be that far from where you started and if you take a different route from the one described, it really doesn't matter. It is best to turn up with a map (or buy one from the excellent visitor centre at High Beach). There are plenty of good-quality gravel tracks in Epping Forest, although these may become muddy in the depths of winter or after prolonged rain. There are several short hills, some of which are quite steep.

On your bikes!

1. With your back to the Kings Oak pub by the High Beach Visitor Centre, turn right. At the T-junction (with a gravel parking strip opposite), turn right then left on to a track by a barrier and wooden posts. At a second road go straight across 'Emergency Access'. Ignore a left turn after 150m.

2. At the busy A121 go straight ahead (**TAKE CARE**) then shortly at a T-junction of tracks turn right. At the next major track junction, with a tall, wooden fence ahead and a metal barrier across access to the road to your right, turn left.

3. Cross a minor road (there is a 'Give Way' sign to the right). The next $^1/_4$ mile is noisy, running parallel with the B1393. Cross this road straight ahead. At a T-junction after 275m (with silver birches to your left), turn right.

4. Go through car parks either side of the B172 and past a 'Jack's Hill' signboard. **Easy to miss**: after $^1/_2$ mile, on a gentle descent, take the first broad track on the right. Descend then climb. Go through a car park and diagonally left across the busy A121 (**TAKE CARE**).

GREATER LONDON

Epping Forest Ride **20**

5. Follow another downhill stretch, climb up through a car park and cross the road past a pond. Go past a second pond then after ¼ mile, on a gentle descent shortly after a large grass clearing on the left, take the next right by a white post with a horseshoe sign.

6. Cross the busy A104 (**TAKE CARE**), go through a bridle gate then turn right on a minor road (this is a no through road, without traffic). At the T-junction, with a car park and tea hut to the right, turn left then right on to a broad track with 'Emergency access' barrier.

7. Lots of ups and downs. Ignore a right turn on a wide track by a small triangle of grass with trees on it. At the T-junction with the next road turn left to return to the Kings Oak pub/visitor centre.

Refreshments: Kings Oak pub and cafe at start. Several pubs (and odd tea wagons!) dotted around Epping Forest.
Bike hire and repairs: Go Further Cycling in southern forest, near Chingford, for hire, spares and repairs.
Public transport and bike links: Several (Central) underground stations on outskirts of forest; Loughton is closest to the start (2 miles away). Bikes permitted on above-surface underground trains outside of rush hour. Roding Valley, closest mainline station, 4 miles away. Cycle routes from Lee Valley; route is on National Cycle Network (NCN) 12.
Parking: Several paid car parks in Epping Forest, one at start.
Maps and guides: OS Landranger 167 & 177, Explorer 174.
Website: *www.visiteppingforest.org*

101

Ride 21 Lee Navigation: Waltham Abbey to Islington

Start
Near Bridge 42, Waltham Abbey (51.6868, -0.0118, TL 375005)

Finish
Islington Tunnel, Islington (51.5333, -0.1029, TQ 317833)

Distance
14 miles/22.5km.

Category
Canal towpaths.

Other facilities

NB In London along the Regent's Canal, the towpath is narrow under the low bridges – ring your bell, slow down and be prepared to meet people and give way. This section is popular both with walkers and cyclists.

Linking Islington in Central London with Waltham Abbey in Hertfordshire, the Lee Navigation is a green corridor offering one of the best escapes from city to country. At the southern end there are several canals: the Regent's Canal, which emerges from Islington Tunnel, is part of the Grand Union Canal, leading to its junction with the River Thames at Limehouse Basin; the Hertford Union Canal links Regent's Canal with the Lee Navigation alongside Victoria Park – and then there is the Limehouse Cut. North of Hackney/Stratford and the Olympic Zone there is just the Lee Navigation, winding its way north past Hackney Marshes, covered in over 80 football pitches. The path is wide and there are no low bridges, by contrast with the route in London itself. To look at the map one would imagine seeing a succession of vast reservoirs up the valley. As it is, the towpath lies below the surrounding embankments for the reservoirs, and they remain hidden. There are lots of pubs and a couple of cafes along the way, so you have plenty of reasons for taking this ride at a leisurely pace.

On your bikes!

1. From Waltham Abbey follow the towpath south, with the canal to your left. Pass under the M25, go past the Greyhound pub then Enfield Lock.

2. After 6 miles you will come to the Stonebridge Lock cafe. After a further 2 miles there is another cafe at the north end of Springfield Park.

3. Go past the many football fields that cover Hackney Marshes.

4. About 12 miles south of Waltham Abbey, and just south of Hackney Wick, you will need to turn off the Lee Navigation on to the Hertford Union Canal to continue south to Limehouse Basin or west to Islington on Regent's Canal. This point is by the Olympic site, marked by a three-way sign. Turn right, signposted 'Hertford Union, Victoria Park'.

5. Pass alongside Victoria Park then at the T-junction* with Regent's Canal you can: **(a)** turn left for 1.5 miles to Limehouse Basin and the Thames, **(b)** turn right for 2.5 miles for Islington, as far as the tunnel (at the junction of Noel Road, Danbury Street and Graham Street).

* Remember this point for your return trip as it is easy to miss.

Refreshments: Pubs at regular intervals all along the towpath. Stonebridge Lock cafe, Tottenham. Springfield Park Cafe, Upper Clapton.
Bike hire and repairs: Santander Cycles dock at Graham Street, near Islington tunnel; several bike shops in Islington.
Public transport and bike links: Waltham Cross station, $^3/_4$ mile from start; several stations close to canal; Liverpool Street is London terminal for stations along the ride. Angel underground station, 300m from end; King's Cross St Pancras 1 mile from end.
Parking: Gunpowder Mills or Fishers Green car park at Waltham Abbey (both paid). Enfield Lock, south of M25. Paid car parks in Islington and near King's Cross – this may take you into Congestion Charge area; ride ends within London's ULEZ.
Maps and guides: OS Landranger 166, 176 & 177, Explorer 173 & 174; a London street map may be more useful.
Website: *www.sustrans.org.uk/find-a-route-on-the-national-cycle-network/london-docklands-and-lea-valley*

GREATER LONDON

Lee Navigation: Ride 22
Hertford to Waltham Abbey

Many of the best traffic-free cycling routes in and near London use the towpaths of the waterways that radiate from the capital – these include the Grand Union Canal in the west of London, the Thames to the south-west and the Thames estuary east from Greenwich. The surface of the Lee Navigation towpath has been upgraded to a very high standard – if only all canal towpaths were as good! The whole Lee Valley (or Lea Valley, both spellings are used – take your pick) has become one of the best areas for recreational cycling to the north of London. The ride described here follows the Lee Navigation from its northern terminus in Hertford eastwards through the attractive town of Ware before taking a more southerly course past Cheshunt to Waltham Abbey. This is only a suggested turnaround point: you may wish to do a much shorter ride going only as far as Ware or the pub at Dobb's Weir, or perhaps you may wish to push on further right into London, joining the Thames near Limehouse Basin.

Refreshments: Lots of choice in Hertford, Ware and Waltham Abbey. Jolly Fisherman pub, Crown pub south of Ware; Rye House pub, Rye House; Fish & Eels pub, Dobb's Weir.
Bike hire and repairs: Hertford Cycle Hub, at start, for spares, repairs and hire. Lee Valley Canoe Cycle at Broxbourne (step 4).
Public transport and bike links: Hertford East station, 150m from Lee Navigation near start. Waltham Cross station 3/4 mile from finish. Several stations in between start and end. Lee Navigation can be followed to Limehouse Basin in London.
Parking: Hartham Lane and Hartham Common paid cark parks near start; Royal Gunpowder Mills or Fishers Green car park at Waltham Abbey (both paid).
Maps and guides: OS Landranger 166, Explorer 174.
Website: www.sustrans.org.uk/find-a-route-on-the-national-cycle-network/london-docklands-and-lea-valley

On your bikes!

1. From the Hartham Leisure Centre in Hertford follow 'National Cycle Network Route 61, Ware' signs on the cycle path across the recreation ground, cross Bridge 69 over the canal by the lock-keeper's cottage and turn left along the towpath of the Lee Navigation.

2. After 2 miles, at the road junction in Ware at the end of the towpath, bear right and use the traffic islands (**take care**) to cross the busy road straight ahead to rejoin the towpath.

3. Follow this excellent towpath for 5 miles to the Fish & Eels pub at Dobb's Weir. Beyond here the path quality varies: parts are excellent but there are also some short, rougher stretches.

4. After 1.5 miles go past the Lee Valley Boat Centre and the Crown pub.

5. Continue for a further 6 miles to Waltham Abbey. You will know you are here as it is just after Waltham Town Lock, at Bridge 42. It is suggested you turn around at this point but you may wish to continue south towards London.

Start
Hartham Leisure Centre, Hertford
(51.8001, -0.0766, TL 327130)

Finish
Near Bridge 42, Waltham Abbey
(51.6868, -0.0118, TL 375005)

Distance
14 miles/22.5km.

Category
Canal towpaths, sometimes rough.

Other facilities

NB Care should be taken crossing the A1170 in Ware – use the cycle facility.

103

TRAFFIC-FREE CYCLE TRAILS SOUTH EAST ENGLAND

North of London

1. Black Park
2. Wendover Woods
3. Icknield Way Trail: Princes Risborough to Wendover
4. Ashridge Estate
5. Grand Union Canal: Hemel Hempstead to Tring Reservoir
6. Nickey Line: Harpenden to Hemel Hempstead
7. Heartwood Forest
8. Ayot Greenway
9. Alban Way: Hatfield to St Albans
10. Cole Green Way
11. Grand Union Canal: Milton Keynes to Leighton Buzzard
12. Milton Keynes to Winslow
13. Milton Keynes: Ouse Valley Trail
14. Milton Keynes: Willen Lake and Caldecotte Lake
15. Grand Union Canal: Milton Keynes to Cosgrove
16. The Clay Way
17. John Bunyan Trail, Bedford
18. The University Way (Bedford to Sandy)
19. The Letchworth Greenway
20. Ashwell Street Byway
21. Grafham Water
22. Fen Drayton
23. Wimpole Estate
24. E2 and the Gog Magog Hills
25. Waterbeach to Cambridge along the River Cam
26. Wicken Fen
27. Haddenham Horseshoe
28. Peterborough and Ferry Meadows Country Park

North of London

04

NORTH OF LONDON

North of London

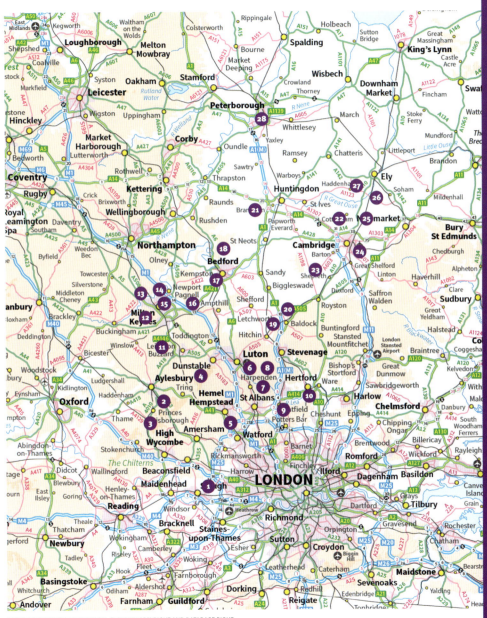

105

Ride 1 **Black Park**

Start/finish
Lakeside cafe,
Black Park
(51.5366, -0.5493,
TQ 007830)

Distance
4 miles/6.5km.

Category
Tarmac paths,
forestry tracks,
grassy bridleway.

Other facilities

If the heathland, tall conifers and sweeping lake of Black Park seem familiar, it is perhaps because they have been the stars of the show in many television programmes and films, thanks to neighbouring film studio Pinewood. The landscaped park was once royal hunting grounds, but now with Go Ape, orienteering courses, fishing and miles of trails to explore, it is the perfect family day out. Some areas of the park are out of bounds to cyclists (the north shore of the lake, for example) but there are miles of well-surfaced trails to explore, as well as mountain bike tracks.

On your bikes!
1. From the cafe on the south side of the lake, follow the gravel path north along the lake. After 150m, turn right and after 250m, at a junction of paths, turn right.

2. After 350m, at another path junction, turn left. After 500m, the trail reaches the park corner; continue on it as it turns left. After 250m, take the right fork.

3. Continue on the bridleway to the north-eastern corner of the park and then turn left. After 550m, turn left to head back towards the lake. After 300m, turn left then almost immediately right. After 60m, turn right. Turn left by the car park, and then left to return to the side of the lake.

4. You can go either way around the lake to return to the start, but this is the most popular area of the park and you may have to dismount. There are many more miles of trails around Black Park to explore, and waymarked trails are being developed; you can also cross the A4007 road to explore the trails in neighbouring Langley Park.

Refreshments: Cafe at start.
Bike hire and repairs: Bike hire from Go Ape (near car park); spares and repairs from Stows Cycles, near Slough station.
Public transport and bike links: Slough station, 3 miles away; (on- and off-road) National Cycle Network (NCN) Route 61 connects Slough to Langley Park, next to Black Park. Beeches Cycleway, 12-mile route that links Black Park, Stoke Common, Burnham Beeches and Dorney Lake.
Parking: Paid parking near lake.
Maps and guides: OS Landranger 176, Explorer 172.
Website: *countryparks.buckscc.gov.uk/black-park*

NORTH OF LONDON

Wendover Woods Ride 2

There are very few Forestry England holdings of any size in the nearby area immediately to the north and west of London. Wendover Woods are the one exception and are the only woodlands in the area with a waymarked trail aimed at recreational family cycling. There are some wonderful views as the car park and (excellent) cafe at the start of the ride are very close to the highest point of the Chiltern Hills. The woodland is mainly broadleaf so there is a fantastic display of bluebells in the late spring, and a glorious riot of colour in the autumn as the trees start to lose their leaves. The only downside to this otherwise perfect combination is that with the starting point at the top of the hill, the route starts off with a long descent and finishes with a long climb back up.

On your bikes!

1. From the Wendover Woods car park continue past the cafe on the tarmac road towards the exit. After 180m keep an eye out for a turning to the right by a tall wooden post with a purple arrow (Firecrest Trail). This is the start of the family cycle route.

2. Gentle descent with great views to the right. After $^1/_3$ mile at a major track junction where the purple trail turns sharp right, either continue straight ahead for the main route or turn right for the shortcut route, avoiding one big hill.

3. After a further $^2/_3$ mile, at a track crossroads, turn right (signs will tell you where you can't go) to continue downhill. At a second crossroads, with a wide stone forestry road at the bottom of a much steeper section, turn right uphill, climbing steadily and steeply.

4. At a T-junction with 'Short Cut' signposted to the right, turn left for the main route (or right for the shortcut). At the next major track junction, turn right uphill then at another T-junction turn left for the main route or right for the shortcut.

5. The track surface becomes rougher. After $^1/_3$ mile, at a fork on the descent bear right. At a T-junction by wooden benches bear left. After a further $^1/_3$ mile, immediately after a wooden barrier by a turning circle with a grass 'roundabout', bear left past wooden fitness equipment for the full route (or go straight ahead for the shortcut).

6. Gentle descent. At a fork bear right on the upper track. At a T-junction turn right sharply back on yourself uphill to return to the start.

Refreshments: Excellent cafe at start.
Bike hire and repairs: Chiltern Cycle Hire at OTEC Bikes shop, Halton, 2 miles from start.
Public transport and bike links: Wendover station, 3 miles away; Icknield Way Trail links Wendover to Wendover Woods.
Parking: Paid parking at start.
Maps and guides: OS Landranger 165, Explorer 181.
Website: www.forestryengland.uk/wendover-woods

Start/finish
Information Centre, Wendover Woods (51.7726, -0.7131, SP 889090)

Distance
6-mile/10km circuit.

Category
Waymarked forestry tracks.

Other facilities

NB *There are also plenty of testing mountain bike trails in the nearby Aston Hill woods. There is a Forestry England policy of trying to keep family cyclists and experienced mountain bikers apart, so if you are super-fit and feel you have not been tested by the routes in Wendover Woods, why not try Aston Hill woods? The site has been badly affected by ash dieback so check* www.rideastonhill.co.uk *before you visit.*

107

Ride 3 Icknield Way Trail: Princes Risborough to Wendover

Start
Whiteleaf Golf Club, Princes Risborough (51.7314, -0.8112, SP 822043)

Finish
Roundabout of South Street and Pound Street, Wendover (51.7617, -0.7445, SP 867078)

Distance
7 miles/11km.

Category
Tarmac roads, grassy bridleways, forest tracks.

Other facilities

The Icknield Way was an ancient trackway from Norfolk to Wiltshire; much of it has been lost under the tarmac of modern roads now. There is, however, the Icknield Way Trail, from Bledlow to Roudham Heath, for cyclists and horse riders; the route follows bridleways, byways and, where necessary, roads. The meandering, wooded section between Princes Risborough passes ancient monuments and the prime minister's country retreat, and offers panoramic views of the Chiltern Hills. You will need to negotiate short road sections if you want to visit the centre of Wendover.

On your bikes!

1. The trail begins near Whiteleaf Golf Club; take the bridleway that turns right off the road just before the clubhouse, not the bridleway at the end of the road. Turn left almost immediately to follow the trail through woods and up the steep sides of Whiteleaf Hill, where there is a chalk cross and Neolithic barrow near the summit.

2. Descend straight on, ignoring the footpath to the left. At the bottom of the woods, turn left on a bridleway on the field edge, rather than continuing on to the car park. At the field end, turn left on to a bridleway through the woods, continuing straight on to Longdown Farm.

3. Cross the road and turn right on to the bridleway through Pulpit Wood. At the bridleway crossroads, continue straight on to reach Missenden Road. Cross the road and turn left on to a bridleway that goes alongside the road; by the entrance to Chequers, it turns right to continue to run beside the road.

4. The bridleway emerges at the entrance of Buckmoorend Farm Shop (a useful refreshment stop) – **take care** when crossing the farm lane to continue straight on. After 300m, at the edge of the woods, turn right to follow the bridleway for just over 1 mile, to emerge at the houses at Little Hampden Common. Turn right for 50m, looking for a bridleway that turns left in front of the houses.

108

Icknield Way Trail: Princes Risborough to Wendover — Ride 3

5. Where the bridleway emerges from the woods at a field edge, there is a junction of paths; ignore the bridleway to the left on the farm track and continue straight on, through woods. At the T-junction, turn left towards Dunsmore. Continue straight on, on the no through road.

6. After 250m, pass the last of the houses and continue straight on, on the bridleway. After 400m, turn right and continue straight on to emerge on Smalldean Lane.

7. The traffic-free section of the trail finishes, but you can turn left and follow the quiet Smalldean Lane for 1/2 mile, and then on to the bridleway that runs parallel to the A413 main road. When you reach the road, turn right to cross the A413 and continue straight on to reach the centre of Wendover.

Refreshments: Plenty of choice in Wendover; clubhouse at Whiteleaf Golf Club.
Bike hire and repairs: Chiltern Cycle Hire at OTEC Bikes shop, Halton, 2 miles from end. Risboro' Car & Cycle Parts, for spares and repairs, 2 miles from start.
Public transport and bike links: Monks Risborough station, 1.5 miles from start; Wendover station, 150m from end.
Parking: Free Whiteleaf Cross car park (near step 2); limited on-street parking in Monks Risborough. Paid street parking and car parks in Wendover.
Maps and guides: OS Landranger 165, Explorer 181.
Website: icknieldwaytrail.org.uk

© SHUTTERSTOCK/STEPHEN TUCKER

Ride 4 **Ashridge Estate**

Start/finish
Ashridge Estate cafe, Ringshall
(51.8077, -0.5938)
SP 970130

Distance
5 miles/8km &
2-mile/3km spur.

Category
Estate paths, woodland tracks.

Other facilities

Comprising over 5,000 acres of woodlands, commons, downland and farmland, the Ashridge Estate runs along the main ridge of the Chiltern Hills from Berkhamsted to Ivinghoe Beacon. The main focal point of the estate is the granite monument erected in 1832 in honour of the 3rd Duke of Bridgewater, father of inland navigation, who was nicknamed 'the Canal Duke'. The ride starts from this mighty monument (which you can climb) and descends through broadleaf woodland on a series of bridleways marked with blue arrows. This is just one of many rides that could be devised in the estate. Be warned, however, that these are woodland tracks rather than specially built cycle trails, so the going can become muddy in winter and after prolonged rain. Mountain or gravel bikes are recommended.

Refreshments: Cafe at start.
Bike hire and repairs: Cycle shops in Tring and Berkhamsted, 4 miles from start.
Public transport and bike links: Tring station, 2 miles from start.
Parking: Free parking at start and elsewhere on estate; donations requested.
Maps and guides: OS Landranger 165, Explorer 181; free cycle map from visitor centre.
Website: www.nationaltrust.org.uk/ashridge-estate

On your bikes!

1. With your back to the cafe and facing the Bridgewater monument, turn left on a broad tarmac path which soon becomes a wide track signposted with a blue arrow for 'Bridleway'.

2. Ignore a first left signposted 'No horses, no bikes'. After 275m of steep descent, at an obvious fork of tracks bear left on the upper track. At a track T-junction by a telephone pole, turn left uphill.

3. Shortly go straight ahead past a house with a high surrounding hedge on your left. Continue in the same direction.

4. Long, gentle descent. At the B4506 go straight ahead (**take care**) on to the track opposite signposted 'Berkhamsted Common'. Continue descending on a slightly rougher track.

5. At a fork after $^2/_3$ mile bear right, then at the crossroads shortly after passing a house to the left turn right uphill on a broad stone 'drive' (blue arrow).

© SHUTTERSTOCK/SARAHHOWARDPHOTOGRAPHY

Ashridge Estate Ride 4

6. At the next crossroads of tracks (with a red-brick barn 50m ahead) turn right on a broad stone track (blue arrow). Shortly, at a 'Little Coldharbour Farm' sign, bear right away from the stone track on to a narrower track (blue arrow) and soon fork right again.

7. Follow the flat singletrack trail through woodland. At times there are roots and there will be mud after rain. At the junction with the B4506, go straight ahead on to the lane opposite signposted 'Aldbury, Tring'. Go past Base Camp on the right and a car parking area on the left. Just before '40mph' speed limit signs turn right on to a track signposted 'Bridgewater Monument'.

8. After 175m, at a crossroads of tracks turn right then at the house, with its high surrounding edge, turn left to rejoin the outward route, soon forking right. After a gentle descent, the last $1/4$ mile back to the monument is steep and you may prefer to push.

Duncombe Terrace Route
There is also a 2-mile there-and-back ride on a broad stone track that heads due north from the Bridgewater monument through magnificent beechwood woodland as far as the Ivinghoe Beacon road, offering fine views west towards Wendover Woods.

111

Ride 5 Grand Union Canal: Hemel Hempstead to Tring Reservoir

Start
Nash Mills, Hemel Hempstead
(51.7275, -0.4526, TL 070043)

Finish
Lower Icknield Way, Marsworth
(51.8185, -0.6670, SP 920142)

Distance
12 miles/19km.

Category
Canal towpaths, sometimes rough.

Other facilities

The Grand Union Canal connects London to Birmingham, but it would take a brave person to jump on their bike at one end and imagine a straightforward ride to the other. There is an enormous variety of surfaces you will encounter, from very rough and rutted paths to fine, smooth gravel; some parts may be overgrown with vegetation and others are very narrow, and also there are barriers to keep out motorbikes. So it is sensible to pick and choose the best bits. Parts of this ride, for example through Berkhamsted, are as good as it gets. However, even on a ride like this there are short, rougher sections, so be prepared for these. The ride runs alongside Tring Summit, the highpoint of the canal between London and the Midlands; to the north it drops down to Milton Keynes and to the south towards London. You won't be stuck for refreshments on this ride, as there are cafes at both ends and many pubs along the way, especially through Berkhamsted.

Refreshments: Trail starts next to Red Lion pub, finishes at Waters Edge restaurant. Several waterfront pubs en route.
Bike hire and repairs: Cycle shops in Tring and Hemel Hempstead. Lovelo Cycle Works and (children's) The Little Bike Company, 200m off-route in Berkhamsted.
Public transport and bike links: Apsley rail station, 300m from Apsley Waterside & Marina. Tring station, 3 miles from end (on route).
Parking: Limited road parking on A4251, near Nash Mills; paid car park at trail end in Marsworth.
Maps and guides: OS Landranger 165 & 166, Explorer 181 & 182.
Website: *canalrivertrust.org.uk/places-to-visit/tring-marsworth*

On your bikes!

1. From the Red Lion pub (by Nash Mills, at the southern edge of Hemel Hempstead) follow the canal towpath north-west towards Berkhamsted. Go past Apsley Waterside & Marina.

2. Go past the Fishery Inn then, after 1 mile, go past another marina and the Three Horseshoes pub.

3. The path improves through Berkhamsted as you pass several pubs and information boards about the history of the canal and the town itself.

4. The surface is good as far as Cow Roast Lock. After this the path becomes narrower and at times overgrown. This is the summit section of the canal.

5. The towpath improves again at Bulbourne as the canal starts its descent. It is suggested that you go as far as Marsworth, where there are plenty of places to grab a bite to eat.

NORTH OF LONDON

Nickey Line: Ride 6
Harpenden to Hemel Hempstead

The Nickey Line follows the course of the old railway gently uphill from Harpenden to Adeyfield Road in Hemel Hempstead (near the town hall). The name may have come from an abbreviation of 'funicular', referring to the steep gradients along the line, or from 'knickerbockers', either because the railway navvies wore such garments or because the line was considered half-size, being only singletrack. The Nickey Line was opened in 1877 as the result of a proposal by the businessmen of Hemel Hempstead to link the straw plait trade in the town with the hatmakers of Luton. It carried passengers until 1947 and freight until 1979.

On your bikes!

1. Join the railway path off Park Hill, Harpenden and turn right uphill. (Remember where you join the path for your return; the path continues for a further 1/2 mile to Hollybush Lane, but access is via a long set of steps.) Climb gently then descend. At the roundabout after 1.5 miles, cross the B487 and A5183 **with great care** following 'National Cycle Network Route 57' signs.

2. After 3/4 mile at the fork bear left to avoid steps. At the road turn right then left.

3. After a further 3/4 mile recross the B487 then go through the tunnel under the M1.

4. After 2 miles the trail ends abruptly at Eastman Way on the edge of Hemel Hempstead. It is suggested you turn around at this point to return. The Nickey Line does continue on for another mile, but there is no level, non-barriered access near the end and you have to follow the road briefly through the busy industrial estate.

Refreshments: Lots of choice in Harpenden and Hemel Hempstead.
Bike hire and repairs: Bike shops in Harpenden and Hemel Hempstead, including Riders in Gear next to Harpenden station.
Public transport and bike links: Harpenden station, 1 mile from start; Hemel Hempstead station, 3 miles from end.
Parking: On road parking near start and finish.
Maps and guides: OS Landranger 166, Explorer 182; free cycle map available (see website).
Website: www.nickeyline.org

Start
Park Hill, Harpenden
(51.8220, -0.3661, TL 127150)

Finish
Eastman Way, Hemel Hempstead
(51.7707, -0.4445, TL 074091)

Distance
7 miles/11km.

Category
Railway paths.

Other facilities

Ride 7 Heartwood Forest

Start/finish
Heartwood Forest car park, St Albans (51.7829, -0.3086, TL 168107)

Distance
4 miles/6.5km.

Category
Forestry tracks, muddy bridleways.

Other facilities

Heartwood Forest, on the outskirts of St Albans, is England's largest new native forest, although it incorporates pockets of much older woodland. A popular destination for walkers, horse riders and cyclists, there are miles of bridleways to explore. Spring, when bluebells carpet the forest floor, is a great time to visit, but whenever you go you are likely to encounter muddy trails. A loop is suggested, which takes in some of the well-established woodland, but you can choose to explore further. You may encounter horse hop barriers on the bridleways.

Refreshments: Pubs in Sandridge, 300m from start.
Bike hire and repairs: Bike shops in St Albans.
Public transport and bike links: St Albans station, 2.5 miles from start.
Parking: Free car park at start.
Maps and guides: OS Landranger 166, Explorer 182.
Website: heartwood.woodlandtrust.org.uk

On your bikes!

1. Take the main bridleway from the back of the car park, heading north-west towards the Magical Wood. After 650m, turn right and at a path junction, left and almost immediately left again to remain on the bridleway.

2. After 550m, at the corner of old woodland, turn left to follow the edge of the woods – you meet the main bridleway from the car park. Turn right. After 600m, turn right.

3. After ³/₄ mile, turn right and follow the bridleway as it bends right around established woodland. Continue straight on to return to the woodland corner (step 2). Continue on the main bridleway, but turn left to return to the forest car park.

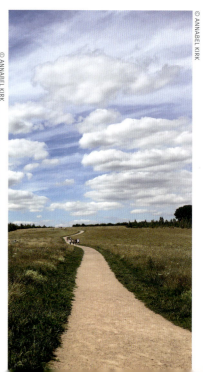

NORTH OF LONDON

Ayot Greenway   Ride 8

A short ride along the course of the old Luton, Dunstable and Welwyn Junction railway from Wheathampstead east to the minor road south of Welwyn, with some lovely, wooded sections. Many men were employed building the line, but the hardest workers would have been the navvies. A day's work for two of them would be to shovel 20 tons of rock and earth into 14 horse-drawn wagons. Although the work was hard, the pay, ranging between 15 and 22 shillings per week, was better than that of farm workers, so many men left the farms to work on the railway. It took two years to complete the stretch of the line between Luton and Hatfield, and the first excursion over the new section ran to London. The cheapest return fare from Luton to London was two shillings and sixpence (12.5p!).

On your bikes!

1. From Miller & Carter's The Bull on the High Street, cross the bridge over the river and after 50m turn right on to Mount Road, following signs for 'Ayot Greenway, Welwyn Garden City, National Cycle Network Routes 12/57'.

2. Fine, wide, smooth gravel track. Pass through several bridle gates. At the T-junction turn left, 'Ayot Greenway' (remember this spot for the return leg).

3. Gentle climb. At a crossroads of tracks turn right, signposted 'Ayot Greenway'.

4. Lovely gentle climb through mature broadleaf woodland. The traffic-free section ends at its junction with Ayot St Peter Road, a minor road south of Welwyn.

Refreshments: In Wheathampstead or Welwyn, 1.5 miles beyond the end of the trail on minor roads (you will need a map).
Bike hire and repairs: Spares and repairs from Electric Bike Vault, High Street, Wheathampstead. Several cycle shops in Welwyn.
Public transport and bike links: Welwyn Garden City station, 2 miles from trail end. At Ayot St Peter Road end, route joins National Cycle Network (NCN) 12 which offers a (mostly on-road) route into Welwyn, where NCN 61 and NCN 12 meet.
Parking: Free car parks at start (East Lane) and end (Ayot Greenway).
Maps and guides: OS Landranger 166, Explorer 182.
Website: www.sustrans.org.uk/find-a-route-on-the-national-cycle-network/hertfordshire-greenways-wheathampstead-to-ware

Start
Miller & Carter's The Bull, Wheathampstead (51.8133, -0.2933, TL 177141)

Finish
Junction of Ayot Little Green Lane and Ayot St Peter Road, Welwyn (51.8159, -0.2310, TL 220145)

Distance
3.5 miles/5.5km.

Category
Railway paths.

Other facilities

Ride 9 Alban Way: Hatfield to St Albans

Start
Great North Road, Old Hatfield
(51.7691, -0.2164, TL 232093)

Finish
Crossroads of Leyland Avenue, Mentmore Road and Cottonmill Lane, St Albans
(51.7431, -0.3369, TL 149062)

Distance
6.5 miles/10.5km.

Category
Railway paths.

Other facilities

It is well worth exploring this fine wooded railway trail between these two towns, forming part of Route 61 of the National Cycle Network (NCN). The route runs south-west from Old Hatfield to St Albans on a fine gravel path with a deep cutting at the St Albans end. There are short sections on quiet roads at the start and finish and three other road crossings, but none are particularly busy. Opened in 1865 by the Hatfield & St Albans Railway Company, the line was absorbed by the Great Northern Railway in 1883. Passenger services continued until 1951 and freight lines until the late 1960s. In 1985 the line was given a new lease of life when it was converted to a cycleway/footpath. All that is left of Verulamium, once one of the most important Roman towns in Britain, lies to the west of the present city of St Albans. There are the remains of a great amphitheatre and part of an underground heating system. Modern St Albans takes its name from Alban, the first Christian martyr in Britain. The mighty abbey was founded on the hill where he was beheaded.

On your bikes!

1. From the top of Great North Road turn right on to the cycle path just before the bridge over the railway. After ³/₄ mile at a fork bear right to cross the road by Fiddlebridge Industrial Centre. At the road junction turn right then left opposite De Havilland Close.

2. Pass under the subway following 'National Cycle Network Route 61' signs. Turn right to cross the bridge over the A1 then left opposite The Galleria shopping centre to continue along the Alban Way.

3. Move from the town into the countryside, passing a small lake to your left.

4. Cross a road beyond a metal barrier, pass through a residential area and cross Sutton Road.

5. After 1 mile pass under an enormous brick arch. After a further ¹/₂ mile at a T-junction just beyond a red-brick-and-concrete bridge, turn right, signposted 'Abbey Station, City Centre, Harpenden'. The traffic-free trail shortly ends.

Refreshments: Lots of choice in St Albans or Hatfield.

Bike hire and repairs: Several bike shops in Hatfield and St Albans, including Hatfield Cycle Hub, 450m from start and Halfords, 500m from route end.

Public transport and bike links:
Hatfield station, ¹/₂ mile from start; St Albans Abbey station ¹/₂ mile from end.

Parking: On-street parking at start and end.

Maps and guides: OS Landranger 166, Explorer 182.

Website: www.stalbans.gov.uk/walking-and-cycling

Cole Green Way — Ride 10

This is the most rural of the four dismantled railways in Hertfordshire, passing through attractive woodland between the rivers Lee and Mimram, linking Welwyn Garden City and Hertford. The trail follows the course of the old Hertford, Dunstable and Luton line. It was opened in 1858 by the Hertford & Welwyn Junction Railway and carried passengers up to 1951 and freight until 1962. It was acquired by Hertfordshire County Council in 1974 and converted to a walking and riding route.

On your bikes!

1. From the Hertford Town Football Club aim towards, then pass beneath, the large railway viaduct. After 175m bear right at a 'National Cycle Network Route 61' sign, staying on the broad gravel track through woodland.

2. Go past a car park on the right. Exit here if you wish to visit the Cowper Arms pub.

3. Pass through the subway under the A414. Climb past the modern planted woodland on your right.

4. The traffic-free trail ends after a further mile at a T-junction with a road on the eastern edge of Welwyn (at the junction of Black Fan Road with Cole Green Lane). National Cycle Network (NCN) 61 continues on a mixture of quiet streets and cycle paths into Welwyn.

Refreshments: Lots of choice in Hertford and Welwyn; Cowper Arms en route.
Bike hire and repairs: Several bike shops in Welwyn Garden City and Hertford.
Public transport and bike links: Start is 1 mile from Hertford North station; end is 2 miles from Welwyn Garden City station. NCN 61 continues on from start to Hertford town centre, and end to Welwyn.
Parking: Free parking at start; car park en route near Cowper Arms. Limited on-street parking near end.
Maps and guides: OS Landranger 166, Explorer 182 & 194.
Website: www.waretourism.org.uk/ColeGreenWay_1.pdf

Start
Hertford Town Football Club, Hertford (51.7907, -0.0883, TL 319120)

Finish
Junction of Black Fan Road and Cole Green Lane, Welwyn (51.7908, -0.1682, TL 264118)

Distance
4 miles/6.5km.

Category
Railway paths.

Other facilities

Ride 11 Grand Union Canal: Milton Keynes to Leighton Buzzard

Start
Bridge 99, near Willowbridge Marina (51.9775, -0.7160, SP 883318)

Finish
Grove Lock pub, Leighton Buzzard (51.8981, -0.6714, SP 915230)

Distance
7.5 miles/12km.

Category
Canal towpaths.

Other facilities

The Grand Union Canal near Milton Keynes is featured twice in this book: Ride 15 (p124) explores the canal north from the centre of the town along the Broadwalk as far as Cosgrove to the north-west; this ride heads due south from the southern edge of town to Leighton Buzzard. The towpath on the middle section between these two rides has a much poorer surface. By contrast, the recent improvements to the towpath south of Bletchley mean this is one of the best stretches for cycling on the whole canal between London and Birmingham. The excellent quality continues south beyond the centre of Leighton Buzzard for another 1.5 miles to the pub near Grove Lock, then abruptly turns to grass.

On your bikes!

1. From Bridge 99, near Willowbridge Marina in Bletchley/Water Eaton, follow the towpath south with the canal to your right.

2. After 2.5 miles go past the Three Locks pub.

3. After another 2.5 miles, follow 'National Cycle Network Route 6' signs

Refreshments: Lots of choice in Bletchley/Water Eaton, including the Three Locks pub. Lots of choice in Leighton Buzzard: Grove Lock pub; the Globe Inn, just north of Leighton Buzzard.
Bike hire and repairs: Several bike shops in Milton Keynes and Leighton Buzzard.
Public transport and bike links: Bletchley station, 2 miles from start. Leighton Buzzard station, 3 miles from end; trail passes through Leighton Buzzard town centre.
Parking: Free, small car park at start. Free, small car park at Tiddenfoot Waterside Park, 1 mile from Grove Lock.
Maps and guides: OS Landranger 152 & 165, Explorer 192.
Website: www.sustrans.org.uk/find-a-route-on-the-national-cycle-network/grand-union-canal

past the Globe Inn and Wyvern Shipping Co. boat hire just north of Leighton Buzzard town centre.

4. The good-quality towpath continues beyond Leighton Buzzard for a further 1.5 miles as far as the Grove Lock pub.

NORTH OF LONDON

Milton Keynes to Winslow   Ride 12

This nine-mile section of the National Cycle Network (NCN) connects the astonishing urban cycle network of Milton Keynes Redway to the small, attractive old town of Winslow via cycle paths and quiet lanes across the gently undulating Buckinghamshire countryside. The ride starts from near the National Bowl at the distinctive silver star sculpture on the eastern edge of Furzton Lake, and follows the cycle path that runs along Emerson Valley almost to the edge of town. A succession of right of ways have been improved with stone and gravel to create a route that travels almost due south-west to the edge of Winslow, with its handsome red-brick buildings and fine square. There are plenty of refreshments available at several cafes and pubs.

On your bikes!

1. Follow the cycle path around the east side of Furzton Lake towards a tall, silver star sculpture, soon picking up signs for 'National Cycle Network Route 51, Winslow'.

2. Turn left after passing a cricket pavilion on the left, following the path around the cricket pitch/playing field to your left. Shortly after crossing a small stream, turn right (all 'NCN 51' signs).

3. Follow the route along the valley for just over 1 mile. Immediately after passing under the second large concrete bridge, turn sharp left uphill by a tall metal millennium signpost. Follow the cycle path alongside V2 (Tattenhoe Street) under the subway then right alongside H8 (Standing Way).

4. Follow NCN 51 round to the left alongside Buckingham Road then after $^{1}/_{4}$ mile **take care** turning right on to the track (NCN 51) on the other side of the road.

5. Continue in the same direction at several crossroads over the next 3.5 miles. The trail briefly joins the lane network. Follow signs for Swanbourne, then on a sharp left-hand bend after $^{2}/_{3}$ mile bear right on to a no through road by a 'Moco Farm' sign. Shortly, as the farm road swings right, bear left through a gate on to a track.

6. The track turns to tarmac. At a T-junction with a wider road, turn right on the shared-use pavement then shortly right again.

7. The route into Winslow town centre uses several roads and cycle paths but it is well signposted. There are plenty of pubs, cafes and tea rooms.

Refreshments: Lots of choice in Winslow. Furzton Lake pub at start.
Bike hire and repairs: Santander Cycles MK has docking stations around city; closest are Dulverton Drive and Blackmoor Gate. Lots of bike shops in Milton Keynes.
Public transport and bike links: Milton Keynes Central station 2 miles from start; trail uses NCN Route 51, which also connects (off-road) with Milton Keynes centre.
Parking: Free car parks at Furzton Lake; free car parks in Winslow centre.
Maps and guides: OS Landranger 152 & 165, Explorer 192.
Website: www.sustrans.org.uk/find-a-route-on-the-national-cycle-network/route-51

Start
Furzton Lake, Milton Keynes (52.0153, -0.7611, SP 851359)

Finish
Vicarage Road, Winslow (51.9428, -0.8814, SP 770277)

Distance
9 miles /14.5km.

Category
Cycle paths and bridleways.

Other facilities

Ride 13 Milton Keynes: Ouse Valley Trail

Start
Bridge over River Great Ouse, near Stony Stratford Nature Reserve (52.0613, -0.8607, SP 782409)

Finish
Sheppards Close, Newport Pagnell (52.0835, -0.7308, SP 871436)

Distance
7 miles/11.5km.

Category
Riverside and railway paths.

Other facilities

For those who have not yet discovered the secret: Milton Keynes offers more miles of safe and enjoyable family cycling than any other town in the country! There is a vast network of traffic-free cycle tracks through parkland, around lakes and along canal towpaths and disused railways. It is also at a crossroads of the National Cycle Network (NCN): Route 51 passes through Milton Keynes on its way from Oxford to Cambridge, while Route 6 runs south from Derby down to London. The ride described here starts on the western fringes of the town, at the old bridge over the River Great Ouse between Old Stratford and Stony Stratford, running alongside the river for four miles on a tarmac path. You pass through a narrow tunnel through the Iron Trunk Aqueduct, which carries the Grand Union Canal over the River Great Ouse, then beneath the railway viaduct. At New Bradwell the route veers away from the river and joins the course of the dismantled railway through leafy cuttings as far as Newport Pagnell. With the aid of a Redway map (see website), it is easily possible to plan several days out exploring this network of traffic-free trails.

Refreshments: Lots of choice in Old Stratford and Newport Pagnell. Pubs just off route where it crosses Grand Union Canal (follow canal either north or south).
Bike hire and repairs: Several bike shops in Milton Keynes.
Public transport and bike links: Milton Keynes Central station, 6 miles from start (mainly on traffic-free redways). Wolverton station en route, near Bradwell Windmill. On NCN 6 (between London and Threlkeld).
Parking: Limited on-street parking near start and end. Free Nature Reserve and Watermill Lane car parks, near start.
Maps and guides: OS Landranger 152 & 165, Explorer 192 & 207.
Website: *getaroundmk.org.uk/cycling/where-to-ride*

On your bikes!

1. From the bridge over the River Great Ouse on the road between Old Stratford and Stony Stratford, follow the path signposted 'Wildlife Conservation Area, Canal, New Bradwell'; **take care** and use the traffic island if you need to cross the road.

NORTH OF LONDON

Milton Keynes: Ouse Valley Trail Ride 13

2. Stay close to the river (on your left). After almost 1 mile, go through a metal gate, turn left and then shortly, at an offset crossroads with a wide track/drive (there is a large red-brick house to your left), go straight ahead on to a continuation of the path. Go through a narrow tunnel beneath the Iron Trunk Aqueduct (which carries the Grand Union Canal). There are some steps down the other side.

3. Cross a wide, wooden bridge over a side stream and turn left at the T-junction, signposted 'Riverside Walk, New Bradwell', to pass beneath the massive brick railway bridge. After almost 1 mile, at a fork of tracks immediately after crossing a small bridge over a stream, bear right away from the river, signposted 'National Cycle Network Route 6'.

4. Follow 'NCN 6' signs, running alongside a main road (V6), under two large, closely spaced concrete bridges, then turn sharp left, signposted 'Railway Walk, Newport Pagnell'.

5. Join the railway path (near Bradwell Windmill) and follow signs for 'Newport Pagnell'. Cross the Grand Union Canal after 1.5 miles. Stay on the railway path for a further 2 miles. The trail ends at Sheppards Close in Newport Pagnell.

121

Ride 14 Milton Keynes: Willen Lake and Caldecotte Lake

Start/finish
Nipponzan Myohoji Buddhist temple, Willen Lake (52.0555, -0.7249, SP 875405)

Distance
12 miles/20km (approximately 3-mile circuit of Willen Lake, 3-mile circuit of Caldecotte Lake, and 3 miles each way for linking section).

Category
Lakeside and riverside (tarmac) paths.

Other facilities

There is an excellent network of recreational cycle routes around Milton Keynes, including circuits of lakes, tree-lined canal towpaths and well-made paths across parkland. Other surprises include lots of adventure playgrounds. The suggested ride below runs along the valley formed by the River Ouzel, linking Willen Lake and Caldecotte Lake, the two largest expanses of water in Milton Keynes. Willen Lake is also a major centre for water sports, so you will probably see the brightly coloured sails of windsurfers and dinghies on the water. Near to Willen Lake is a Buddhist pagoda and a maze, which are both well worth a visit. The ride takes you past woodland and along the willow trees lining the banks of the river. As you approach Caldecotte Lake you will see the windmill standing on its shores. A complete circuit of the lake, with the chance of refreshment at the Caldecotte Pub & Grill, points you back in the right direction for your return along the river back to the start at Willen Lake.

On your bikes!

1. Join the path at the water's edge near the Japanese-style Nipponzan Myohoji Buddhist temple and turn right under the bridge. Follow the lakeside path around the edge of the lake (with the water to your left), going past the high ropes and adventure area.

2. At the T-junction where the main track continues around the edge of the lake, turn right, following signs for 'Milton Keynes Village and the Ouzel Valley'. For the next 3 miles you are following signs for 'Riverside Walk, Walton Lake and Caldecotte'.

3. Keep the river on your left; do not cross bridges over it for 3 miles. At the T-junction with Simpson Road, turn left then right through the metal height barrier, bearing diagonally right through the car park to pick up signs for 'Caldecotte Lake'.

4. Complete a circuit of the lake – head towards the windmill, keeping the water on your left. Go past the Caldecotte Pub & Grill and the birdwatching point. Stay on the paths closest to the water's edge. At times this is a bit confusing but you'll soon find the right path.

5. On the return follow signs for 'Simpson' and 'Riverside Walk'. At the dam at the northern end of the lake bear right, away from the water, to join a wide cycle path alongside the road.

NORTH OF LONDON

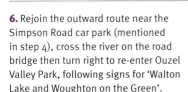

Milton Keynes: Willen Lake and Caldecotte Lake Ride **14**

6. Rejoin the outward route near the Simpson Road car park (mentioned in step 4), cross the river on the road bridge then turn right to re-enter Ouzel Valley Park, following signs for 'Walton Lake and Woughton on the Green'.

7. Keep the river to the right (do not cross it) and stay on the broad tarmac path, following signs for 'Riverside Walk, Woughton on the Green, Woolstones'. Continue in the same direction to join the lakeside path alongside Willen Lake, keeping the water to your left.

8. Follow signs for 'Willen Lake North' and 'Willen Village'. At the north end of the North Lake follow the shoreline round to the left past the Peace Pagoda to return to the start.

Refreshments: Cafe at the Willen Watersports Centre; Lakeside pub, Willen Lake South. Caldecotte Pub & Grill on Caldecotte Lake.
Bike hire and repairs: Adventure Cycle Hire at Willen Lake; Santander Cycles MK bike docking stations at Caldecotte Lake and Willen Lake. Several bike shops in Milton Keynes.
Public transport and bike links: Milton Keynes Central station, 2.5 miles from Willen Lake South (via traffic-free redways); Bow Brickhill station, 600m from Caldecotte Lake.
Parking: Five paid car parks at Willen Lake and two free at Caldecotte Lake; suggested start is near the Peace Pagoda car park.
Maps and guides: OS Landranger 152, Explorer 192.
Website: *getaroundmk.org.uk/cycling/where-to-ride*

© SHUTTERSTOCK/JACKIE MATTHEWS

123

Ride 15 Grand Union Canal: Milton Keynes to Cosgrove

Start
Ouzel Valley Park, Woughton on the Green (52.0349, -0.7230, SP 877382)

Finish
Manor Close, Cosgrove (52.0778, -0.8178, SP 791428)

Distance
11 miles/18km.

Category
Canal towpaths.

Other facilities

This ride gives you a real idea of how much work has gone into the creation of the Redway in Milton Keynes. At one extreme, running four miles north from Woughton on the Green in the heart of town, you have the Broadwalk, one of the finest examples of landscaped, tree-lined, traffic-free cycle trails in the country. At the other end of the spectrum are stretches of the canal towpath lying outside the town boundaries, where no improvement work has been undertaken and the rough surface means that your bones and bikes will get a good shaking. Luckily, these rough sections are a rarity. There is much to enjoy on this ride, from the aforementioned Broadwalk to the wide grass expanses of Great Linford Park, the lovely old buildings in Great Linford itself, the rural vistas as the canal passes out into the countryside and the long mural of a freight train with its diverse load on the canalside wall in Wolverton. Cosgrove is a small, attractive village with two pubs and makes a convenient turn-around point. This being Milton Keynes, there are plenty of options for varying your return journey, although it is recommended that you consult the interactive cycling or Redways map online (see website).

On your bikes!

1. From the entrance to the car park in Woughton on the Green, turn left then right at the road hump on to the yellow gravel track on the other side.

2. Continue in the same direction through parkland, ignoring several left turns until arriving at a red-brick humpback bridge over the canal (Bridge 87). Turn right on the Broadwalk, keeping the canal to your left.

3. Continue north along the Broadwalk parallel with the canal for 3.5 miles following signs for Woolstone, Newlands

124

NORTH OF LONDON

Grand Union Canal: Milton Keynes to Cosgrove Ride 15

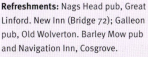

and Willen Park. Keep an eye out for the bridge numbers. At Bridge 78 B (a modern bridge with metal railings), the main wide path swings up and to the right, turning back on itself to cross this bridge over to the west side of the canal. **Remember** this point for the return trip.

4. Proceed north alongside the canal for 1/3 mile, then just before a red-brick bridge at a four-way signpost turn left, signposted 'Linford Manor Park'. At a crossroads of paths go straight ahead, signposted 'Playing fields', then cross the road on to High Street.

5. As the road swings left by the Nags Head pub turn right through gates into parkland. Pass between old houses, go past the church then a collection of large stones. Rejoin the canal towpath, which shortly changes sides.

6. Follow the canal over a variety of surfaces for a further 4.5 miles to Cosgrove, passing the following

Refreshments: Nags Head pub, Great Linford. New Inn (Bridge 72); Galleon pub, Old Wolverton. Barley Mow pub and Navigation Inn, Cosgrove.
Bike hire and repairs: Several bike shops in Milton Keynes. Santander Cycles MK bike dock, 1 mile from start.
Public transport and bike links: Milton Keynes Central station 3 miles from start (via traffic-free Redways).
Parking: Free car park at start. On-street parking near end.
Maps and guides: OS Landranger 152, Explorer 192 & 207.
Website: getaroundmk.org.uk/cycling/where-to-ride

landmarks: New Inn (Bridge 72), a long, black-and-white mural with pictures of freight trains, the Galleon pub, the Iron Trunk Aqueduct over the River Great Ouse, the junction with the Buckingham Arm and the Navigation Inn and Barley Mow pub at Cosgrove.

Ride 16 The Clay Way

Start
Ridgmont station, Ridgmont
(52.0265, -0.5942, SP 965374)

Finish
Stagsden Road, Bromham Mill
(52.1450, -0.5249, TL 010507)

Distance
14 miles/22.5km
(9 miles/14km from Cranfield).

Category
Tarmac access roads, grass-topped farm tracks, stone-topped bridleways.

Other facilities

The Clay Way follows a clay ridge through the Marston Vale, offering fine views of Bedfordshire's rolling farmland and woods, and also in the distance Milton Keynes and Cranfield airport. The trail is a mixture of tarmac tracks, stone-topped bridleways and muddy farm tracks; rutted tracks across clay fields may be difficult to tackle in wet, wintry weather. There are barriers and gates to negotiate. The trail follows roads for approximately one mile through Cranfield; if you wish to avoid this, you can start the route from the bridleway off Crane Way (step 6). The Clay Way is also part of the John Bunyan Trail.

On your bikes!

1. The trail starts 250m from Ridgmont station; turn right from the station. The cycle track forks left just before the roundabout. Do not follow the path across the bridge; turn left and continue straight on, ignoring the path to the right.

2. Follow the farm tracks to Brogborough Farm and turn left to cross the railway. Immediately after the railway bridge, the tarmac track bears left; stay straight ahead towards the woods and ruins of the Round House. After the Round House, the track bends to the left.

3. Take care when crossing Bedford Road; cross the A421 via the footbridge. Follow the lane for 600m, until its end. Continue straight on, on farm tracks; after another 600m, the track turns right and then left on a field edge, next to some woods.

4. At the field end, go through a gap in the hedge to continue straight on through the woods. Emerge into another field, and after 350m turn right. Turn right when you meet the farm track.

5. Follow Woodend Road, which becomes Court Road, for $3/4$ of a mile. Turn right on to Rectory Lane (towards the cemetery). Take the stone-topped

The Clay Way Ride 16

bridleway as it forks left off the road; continue on when the track becomes Holywell Road.

6. Turn right on to Bedford Road and follow it for 550m to where it meets Crane Way; turn left then immediately right on to a bridleway.

7. Follow the bridleway; turn right on Partridge Piece road and then left on to the farm track towards Moat Farm. Continue straight on, ignoring a bridleway to the left. When you reach a T-junction, turn left on to the bridleway.

8. Ignoring bridleways to the left and right, stay straight on for 1.5 miles to reach Bourne End Farm. Turn left at Bourne End Farm. After ¾ mile, turn right on to a bridleway; follow it for nearly 1.5 miles to Hay Lane. Turn right and immediately left, on to a bridleway past woods.

Refreshments: Cafe at Ridgmont station. Pubs and cafes in Cranfield. Cafe at Bromham Mill. Worth making a short detour into Bourne End to visit BikeBus cyclist cafe.
Public transport and bike links: Starts at Ridgmont station; Bedford station, 2.5 miles from end.
Parking: Free car park at Ridgmont station (height-restricted entrance). On-street parking in Cranfield and near end in Bromham.
Maps and guides: OS Landranger 153, Explorer 192 & 208.
Website: *britishpilgrimage.org/portfolio/john-bunyan-trail*

9. Cross Spring Lane and continue straight on, on a bridleway that passes the golf course and along the edge of Hanger Wood. **Take care** when crossing the busy A421 main road, and continue straight on, on a bridleway by houses. The route emerges on Stagsden Road near Bromham Mill.

127

Ride 17 John Bunyan Trail Bedford

Start
Moot Hall, Elstow
(52.1159, -0.4687,
TL 049475)

Finish
Roundabout on
A600/Bedford
Road, Shefford
(52.0453, -0.3467,
TL 135398)

Distance
8 miles/13km.

Category
Tarmac access
roads, grass-
topped farm
tracks.

Other facilities

John Bunyan, Puritan preacher and author of *Pilgrim's Progress*, was born in Elstow where this trail begins. The John Bunyan Trail is an 81-mile, long-distance circular walking route around Bedfordshire's rolling countryside, devised by the Bedfordshire Ramblers association, visiting places associated with the life of Bunyan. The trail frequently takes advantage of bridleways and byways, so often offers good traffic-free rides for cyclists; The Clay Way (p126) also overlaps with the John Bunyan Trail. The route is divided into 10 sections, and the eight-mile section between Elstow and Shefford is a picturesque ride on generally well-surfaced tracks. There are two short sections on quiet country lanes, and there are gates and barriers to negotiate. If you want to find out more about Bunyan, visit the Bunyan Meeting and Museum in Bedford town centre.

Refreshments: Cafe and pub near start; The Greyhound in Haynes. Pubs and cafes in Shefford, 3/4 mile from end.
Bike hire and repairs: Several bike shops in Bedford.
Public transport and bike links: Bedford St Johns station, 1.5 miles from start.
Parking: On-street parking near start and 600m from end.
Maps and guides: OS Landranger 153, Explorer 193 & 208.
Website: britishpilgrimage.org/portfolio/john-bunyan-trail

On your bikes!

1. From the Moot Hall, turn right and follow the High Street (on-road) for 750m, crossing above the A421 main road. Just after the bridge, turn left on to Medbury Lane.

2. Follow Medbury Lane for nearly 1 mile; this is an access road, so you should encounter little traffic. Where the road ends, continue on as the hard-surfaced trail bends to the right. Continue on to the barrier by the road.

3. Turn right on to the road and after 50m, left on to Elms Lane; again, this is an access road, not a through road. After 700m, past Manor Farm, the road becomes hard-surfaced farm track.

4. Continue to follow the track, ignoring the footpath to the right at Northwood End Farm. The track becomes North Lane, and at the end turn right and immediately left. Follow the road for 200m, turning right on to a track past farm buildings (this is a slight detour from the John Bunyan Trail, which takes a footpath right, further on by the Greyhound Pub).

5. Follow the farm tracks and turn left on the road for 300m. Where the road turns left, two bridleways turn off to the right; take the second one that passes in front of Wood Farm (you are now back on the John Bunyan Trail).

6. Continue on farm tracks for 2 miles, crossing a road. At the roundabout, you can continue on for 3/4 mile, into the centre of Shefford where there are pubs and cafes, but you will have to ride on the road.

NORTH OF LONDON

The University Way (Bedford to Sandy)
Ride 18

Starting from the attractive setting of Bedford's Priory Country Park, with its marina, lakes, the River Great Ouse and a bike hire outlet, the course of this old railway whisks you east towards Sandy through a landscape of rich, arable fields. Shortly after crossing the bridge over the A421 you have the option of following the direct route along the railway or taking a longer route alongside the River Great Ouse. Both join at the cafe at Danish Camp, a fine stopping point with lovely views out over the river. Another attraction along the way is the dovecote at Willington. The railway path continues to the edge of Sandy, just west of the A1. The route into town from here uses a mixture of cycle paths and residential roads, so you may prefer to turn around at the end of the traffic-free section. Heading west from Priory Country Park there is an attractive riverside route right through the centre of Bedford.

On your bikes!

1. From the marina in Priory Country Park, follow signs for 'Willington', 'Sandy', 'National Cycle Network Route 51' and 'Danish Camp' along the course of the old railway. (You may wish to go and see the extraordinary Sikh Gurdwara Temple in Queens Park in the centre of Bedford; there is a waymarked riverside path to Priory Country Park.) The cycle path runs on a yellow gravel path parallel to the service road.

2. After 1.5 miles, cross the bridge over the A421 dual carriageway. Shortly you have a choice to reach the cafe at Danish Camp, via the direct route or the riverside route. Both are attractive – why not try one on the outward trip and the other on your return? If you wish to visit Willington Dovecote and the Crown pub in Willington, take the direct route – there are short sections on-road on this option.

3. Both routes rejoin at Danish Camp. Beyond here there is a short, narrow section of footpath where you will need to walk. Signs indicate the start and finish of this section.

4. If you are with children, it is suggested you turn around after a further 3 miles at the end of the traffic-free section immediately before the A1 dual carriageway bridge. However, if you wish to go on into Sandy, there is a waymarked 1.5-mile route, mainly on cycle paths and residential roads, into the centre of town where there are plenty of refreshments.

Refreshments: Lots of choice in Bedford and Sandy: the Priory Marina pub in Priory Country Park (Bedford), the Crown pub at Willington, cafe at the Danish Camp.
Bike hire and repairs: Adventure Cycle Hire, Priory Country Park. Spares and repairs from Sandy Cycles. Several bike shops in Bedford.
Public transport and bike links: Bedford St Johns station, 1 mile from start, and Bedford station 2 miles; Sandy station, 3 miles from end.
Parking: Paid parking at Priory Country Park; limited on-street parking across the A1 at end.
Maps and guides: OS Landranger 153, Explorer 208.
Website: *www.sustrans.org.uk/find-a-route-on-the-national-cycle-network/university-way*

Start
Priory Country Park, Bedford
(52.1321, -0.4406, TL 068493)

Finish
Before crossing of A1, outside Sandy
(52.1397, -0.3047, TL 161504)

Distance
7 miles/11.5km
(3 miles/5km extra from end of Bedford Riverside paths).

Category
Lakeside paths, railway paths.

Other facilities

Ride 19 The Letchworth Greenway

Start
Standalone Farm,
Wilbury Road,
Letchworth
(waymarker 37),
(51.9868, -0.2399,
TL 210335)

Finish
Blackhorse Road,
Letchworth
(waymarker 25),
(51.9901, -0.2013,
TL 236339) or
Willian village
(waymarker 1),
(51.9574, -0.2196,
TL 224303)

Distance
4 miles/6.5km to
Blackhorse Road; 8
miles/13km to
Willian.

Category
Shared-use paths,
tarmac tracks.

Other facilities

Created to commemorate Letchworth's centenary in 2003, the Letchworth Greenway is a 13.6-mile walking and cycling route around the town's green environs. On occasion, cyclists are diverted on to neighbouring roads, however much of the northern section is traffic-free. The route is easy to follow, with numbered waymarks that correspond with the map (available from website); this rideable section of the Greenway begins at waymarker 37 and finishes at waymarker 25. If you wish, with a short section of road and hike-a-bike you can continue on the Greenway as it joins National Cycle Network (NCN) Route 12; when NCN 12 leaves the Greenway you can follow the national cycle route into Letchworth centre.

On your bikes!

1. The trail starts on the lane that leads to Standalone Farm, a working city farm; follow it but do not turn right towards the farm (unless you want refreshments). Instead, continue straight on to a track junction. Turn right.

2. Follow the well-made track for 350m, crossing Pix Brook; turn left on a trail next to the brook. After 450m, the track bends right away from the stream. Turn right (almost straight on) at a track junction after 400m.

3. Turn right with the track after 100m. After 450m, turn left with the Greenway. Turn left again at the corner of the Grange Recreation Area. After 450m, turn right. Continue on the track, crossing Norton Road. The route curves around the edge of Radwell Meadows; exit the country park through the car park and turn right on to Norton Bury Lane for 70m, then turn left on to a farm track. Continue on the track as it bends to run parallel to the A1(M) motorway.

The Letchworth Greenway Ride 19

4. Take care when crossing Norton Road; continue straight on. When the trail emerges on to Blackhorse Road (an access road through an industrial estate), this traffic-free section of the Greenway ends (for cyclists). However, with 300m of road and a short push section, you can continue on to join NCN 12 which loops back into Letchworth city centre (see step 5).

5. To reach NCN 12, continue along Blackhorse Road. Turn left on to Knap Close and dismount to cross the pedestrian bridge across the railway. Continue on the Greenway to cross under the A1(M). Just after it crosses beneath the motorway, turn right on to a track; this is a public footpath, not a bridleway, so you will have to push your bike for 250m. At a junction with a bridleway, turn right to cross under the motorway again (now back on the Greenway but also on NCN 12). NCN 12 and the Greenway keep company until Manor Wood near Willian (although the cycleway runs parallel to the Greenway along Baldock Lane briefly); here the Greenway continues straight on, but you should turn right to follow NCN 12 into Letchworth centre.

Refreshments: Greenway Cafe at Standalone Farm at start; Two Chimneys pub, $1/2$ mile from start. The Fox and Three Horseshoes pubs at Willian.
Bike hire and repairs: Trisports (near Letchworth Garden City station) and Halfords in Letchworth Garden City.
Public transport and bike links: Letchworth Garden City station $3/4$ mile from start, 1.5 miles from Blackhorse Road and 2 miles from Willian. Baldock station, 1 mile from Blackhorse Road. NCN 12 runs through Letchworth (on- and off-road) linking the north and south Greenway loop with the town centre.
Parking: Parking at Standalone Farm and Radwell Meadows.
Maps and guides: OS Landranger 153 & 166, Explorer 193.
Website: *www.discover-letchworth.com/greenway*

Ride 20 Ashwell Street Byway

Start
Junction of Kingsland Way and Ashwell Street, Ashwell (52.0397, -0.1496, TL 270395)

Finish
Junction of A10 and Royston Road, Melbourn (52.0752, -0.0005, TL 371398)

Distance
7 miles/11km.

Category
Tarmac access roads; grass-topped farm tracks.

Other facilities

This byway (generally closed to motor traffic) follows the route of a Roman road. It offers a variety of surfaces, but is frequently on muddy or grassy tracks, making it the perfect mountain or gravel bike adventure. This pleasant route through the flat farm fields of fenland has little ascent or descent. Ashwell is a picturesque village, with three pubs, a cafe and plenty of historic buildings, including a seventeenth-century guildhall. This route has short sections of access roads, where you may encounter a little traffic.

On your bikes!

1. Start on Kingsland Way, just south of the Three Tuns pub; turn left on to Ashwell Street. The first 100m is road access to the properties, but the trail soon turns to rough, gravel-topped track.

2. Cross Station Road and continue on, along the access road to the caravan park. For 300m you may encounter vehicles accessing the caravan park; the trail then becomes hard-surfaced track turning to rutted, grassy track.

Refreshments: Three pubs and cafe in Ashwell. Two pubs in Melbourn.
Public transport and bike links: Ashwell & Morden station, 1.5 miles south of route (second road crossing); Meldreth station, 1.5 miles from route end.
Parking: On-street parking near start and end.
Maps and guides: OS Landranger 153 & 154, Explorer 209.

3. After a second road crossing, for $1/2$ mile the trail becomes farm access track for several properties. The trail becomes farm tracks.

4. Cross Royston Road and follow the broad, grass-topped bridleway through farm fields. Take care when crossing the A1198 road. The route is again hard-surfaced farm tracks; it finishes on the A10 on the outskirts of Melbourn.

Grafham Water Ride 21

North of London

This well-signposted reservoir route on tracks and quiet roads is very popular, particularly during summer weekends. The trail uses stone and gravel paths with some gentle hills where the trail leaves the waterside. The reservoir was built in 1966 and holds 59 billion litres of water. There is plenty of birdlife as well as attractive woodland stretches. For what is meant to be a reservoir circuit it does spend very little time right by the water!

On your bikes!

1. Begin at the Grafham Water Visitor Centre and head north towards the village of Grafham. After a short shoreside section, the route follows quiet singletrack country roads for a little over 1 mile through Grafham to Hill Farm.

2. The trail follows the reservoir edge around the north but meanders away from the water on the western side.

3. As you reach Perry, turn left to follow the trail, past the Grafham Water Sailing Club. Turn right to emerge on the B661 by the Wheatsheaf pub. Follow the road for 350m (there is a cycle path) and soon after Duberley Close on your left, turn left on to a waymarked track through Plummer Park. Continue on the waterside track to return to the start.

Refreshments: Cafe at start and in Mander Park; Wheatsheaf pub in Perry.
Bike hire and repairs: Hire, spares and repairs from Rutland Cycling (Marlow Park car park).
Public transport and bike links: Closest rail station is Huntingdon, 7.5 miles away (via NCN 51/NCN 12). Trail forms part of (on- and off-road) NCN 12 between London and Peterborough.
Parking: Paid parking at Marlow Park; additional pay car parks at Plummer Park and Mander Park.
Maps and guides: OS Landranger 153, Explorer 225.
Website: *anglianwaterparks.co.uk/grafham-water-park/cycling*

Start/finish
Grafham Water Visitor Centre, Grafham (52.2978, -0.2905, TL 167680)

Distance
8 miles/13km.

Category
Round-reservoir route.

Other facilities

133

Ride 22 Fen Drayton

Start/finish
Fen Drayton car park, Fen Drayton (52.3033, -0.0370, TL 339691)

Distance
3 miles/5km.

Category
Tarmac paths and roads, grassy bridleways.

Other facilities

Once sand and gravel quarries, the lakes of Fen Drayton are now a magnet for birds (and birdwatchers). Bridleways, often muddy and narrow, offer a tranquil circuit around the lakes, and this trail is ideal for gravel bikes. The cycle path next to the Guided Busway provides a traffic-free route back to Cambridge, but your close proximity to buses (though the routes are segregated) means this is perhaps best tackled by confident cyclists.

On your bikes!

1. Take the bridleway between Elney Lake and Oxholme Lake. Turn left on to the Busway cycle path for 600m, and then turn right on to the bridleway by the side of Drayton Lagoon.

2. Cycle along the north edge of Drayton Lagoon. Ignore the footpath to the right at the end of the lagoon, and continue on for another 400m. Turn right, and follow the access road back to the Busway cycle path.

3. If you want to avoid traffic, turn right on the cycle path and then left on to the bridleway between Elney Lake and Oxholme Lake. Otherwise, continue straight on across the cycleway; this is an access road for the nature reserve so you may encounter some traffic. At the bottom of Oxholme Lake, turn right and then right again to return to the start.

Refreshments: Three Tuns pub in Fen Drayton, $1/2$ mile from start (on road). Several pubs and cafes in St Ives (2 miles via Guided Busway).
Bike hire and repairs: Spares and repairs from Richardsons Cycles, St Ives (2 miles via Guided Busway).
Public transport and bike links: Huntingdon station, 9 miles away, although Cambridge station 11.5 miles away via Guided Busway (National Cycle Network Route 51) may be easier.
Parking: Free parking at start.
Maps and guides: OS Landranger 154, Explorer 225.
Website: www.rspb.org.uk/reserves-and-events/reserves-a-z/fen-drayton-lakes

© ROSIE MAHER

NORTH OF LONDON

Wimpole Estate Ride 23

Wimpole Estate is a National-Trust-owned country estate, with an impressive seventeenth-century mansion at its heart. The extensive grounds have been shaped by Britain's most famous landscapers, including Capability Brown. In 2021, the National Trust opened a new 5.5 -mile/8.5-kilometre route that circumnavigates the parkland, farmland and woods of the estate. This shared-use, waymarked trail is well-surfaced and family friendly, but particularly the stretch near Wimpole Hall may be busy with walkers and other trail users. There is an entrance fee (except for National Trust members) to visit the estate, which includes the parklands and garden, house and parking; it is often cheaper to visit in winter.

On your bikes!

1. With Wimpole Hall behind you, turn left towards the estate road (from South Lodge). At the estate road, turn left and then immediately right on to a tarmac track that runs parallel to the road.

2. At the T-junction near Home Farm, turn right and follow the track for nearly $1/2$ mile. Turn left at the (far) corner of the woods.

3. Follow the track along the edge of woodland, crossing the estate road again after $1/2$ mile. The route continues through woodlands, turning to the left.

4. At Horse Common Plantation, take the right fork to turn away from the woods. When the trail rejoins the woodland track, turn right.

5. Turn left to return to Wimpole Hall.

Refreshments: Cafe and restaurant near start.
Public transport and bike links: Shepreth station, 7 miles from start.
Parking: Car parking (included in entrance charge), 500m from start.
Maps and guides: OS Landranger 154, Explorer 209.
Website: www.nationaltrust.org.uk/wimpole-estate/projects/wimpoles-multi-user-trail

Start
Wimpole Hall, Arrington (52.1395, -0.0496, TL 336508)

Distance
5.5 miles/8.5km.

Category
Hard-surfaced, shared-use paths.

Other facilities

Ride 24 E2 and the Gog Magog Hills

Start
Wandlebury Country Park, Cambridge (52.1584, 0.1946, TL 502534)

Finish
West Wickham Road, Horseheath (52.1045, 0.3564, TL 615477)

Distance
8.5 miles/13.5km.

Category
Tarmac byways, grassy bridleways, farm tracks.

Other facilities

The E2 is a European long-distance path running from Ireland to France. This trail, which takes advantage of a small section of the E2 near Cambridge, starts by Wandlebury Country Park, a nature reserve in the chalky Gog Magog Hills on the outskirts of Cambridge. Cycling is not permitted in the park, but it is worth taking time to explore the flowered meadows and Iron Age hill fort of the park, as well as Beech Avenue. This is a gravel or mountain bike ride on rutted farm tracks and muddy singletracks; there are also narrow barriers at points on the route. The trail follows the route of a Roman road on bridleways and byways – although some of the route is on byways open to all traffic, you are unlikely to encounter anything (except possibly farm traffic).

On your bikes!

1. If you start in Wandlebury Country Park, you can either enjoy a stroll through the park with your bike to join the byway near the Beech Avenue or take the shared-use cycle path that runs beside the A1307 main road. After 1/2 mile, turn left on to the byway.

2. Follow the byway to the Roman road; turn right. After 2 miles, cross the A11 using the bridge. Continue straight on, on the bridleway. Continue straight on for another 5 miles, crossing two more roads.

3. Cross the road, and continue straight on for nearly 1.5 miles, now on bridleway.

Refreshments: Old Red Lion pub in Horseheath, 1/2 mile from end; occasional pop-up cafes in Wandlebury Country Park.
Bike hire and repairs: Hire, spares and repairs from Campus Cycle Hub, near A1307, at Addenbrooke's Hospital on outskirts of Cambridge, 2 miles from start (via cycle path).
Public transport and bike links: Shelford rail station, 2.5 miles from start; segregated cycle path by A1307 to Cambridge, 5 miles.
Parking: Paid car park at Wandlebury Country Park.
Maps and guides: OS Landranger 154, Explorer 209 & 210.
Website: www.cambridgeppf.org/pages/category/wandlebury-country-park

NORTH OF LONDON

Waterbeach to Cambridge along the River Cam Ride 25

Oxford has the River Thames and Cambridge has the River Cam; both rivers offer wonderful rides along top-quality towpaths that go right into the heart of each city. If you are coming from outside Cambridge, Waterbeach railway station is a convenient place to start as there is a cycle path to the river; there is also a car park there. Follow the towpath along the banks of the willow-lined River Cam for a chance of spotting the vivid turquoise of a kingfisher. The traffic-free path stops at Jesus Green, but as bikes are such an integral part of life in Cambridge, it is possible to continue with confidence right into the heart of the city to see the magnificent colleges along King's Parade.

On your bikes!

1. From Waterbeach railway station, take the cycle path parallel with the road leading away from the station. After 1/4 mile bear right by the Bridge pub to join the river towpath and turn right (water to your left).

2. Follow the river towpath for 4 miles. At the end of the riverside route, turn left on to the cycle path/pavement on Water Street. Then bear left on to a continuation of Water Street.

3. Shortly turn left opposite the Green Dragon pub to cross a footbridge over the river, and turn right. This joins a quiet residential road for 1/4 mile then becomes a traffic-free path once again alongside the river.

Refreshments: The Bridge pub at Waterbeach. Lots of choice in Cambridge.
Bike hire and repairs: Hire from Rutland Cycling and City Cycles, Cambridge; several cycle shops in Cambridge.
Public transport and bike links: Starts at Waterbeach station; finish 1.5 miles from Cambridge station.
Parking: Paid parking at Waterbeach station; paid city car parks in Cambridge.
Maps and guides: OS Landranger 154, Explorer 209 & 226.

4. It is suggested you go as far as the tennis courts by the river on Jesus Green, just beyond Jesus Green swimming pool. If you wish to continue into the heart of Cambridge, keep following 'National Cycle Network Route 11' signs along a series of quiet streets to emerge at King's Parade.

Start
Waterbeach station, Waterbeach (52.2622, 0.1969, TL 500649)

Finish
King's Parade, Cambridge (52.2051, 0.1179, TL 448584)

Distance
6 miles/10km.

Category
Riverside paths.

Other facilities

137

Ride 26 Wicken Fen

Start/finish
Wicken Fen Visitor Centre, Wicken (52.3104, 0.2919, TL 563705)

Distance
3.5 miles/5.5km or more.

Category
Hard-surfaced tracks.

Other facilities

Wicken Fen is a National Trust nature reserve and attracts some of Britain's rarest birds. With its drove tracks across flat fenland, it is the ideal place for a family cycle ride. National Cycle Network (NCN) Route 11 passes through Wicken Fen, and provides a pleasant link route to Ely, much of it off-road. Facilities at Wicken Fen include a cafe, cycle hire and bird hides. You can also enjoy a boat tour on the lodes (man-made waterways created for navigation and drainage, probably of Roman origin). In addition to the routes recommended by the National Trust (described below), you can also explore the Lodes Way, which offers a largely off-road route to the National Trust's Anglesey Abbey, with its historic country house and working mill, in Lode.

Refreshments: Cafe at start, Maids Head pub in Wicken (and other pubs on Villager Explorer route).
Bike hire and repairs: Bike hire at start; bike shops in Ely.
Public transport and bike links:
NCN 11 runs through Wicken Fen – it connects Ely, Cambridge and Waterbeach (with railway stations); Ely is closest (7.5 miles away).
Parking: Paid car park at start.
Maps and guides: OS Landranger 154, Explorer 226.
Website: www.nationaltrust.org.uk/wicken-fen-nature-reserve

On your bikes!
1. The National Trust recommends three waymarked bike rides around Wicken Fen. The Family Discovery Cycle route is a 3.5-mile, out-and-back route from the visitor centre to Charlie's Hide, taking advantage of the drove tracks. There is also a spur that takes you into Wicken village.

2. The Wildlife Watching Route is an 11-mile loop that takes you across Adventurers Fen, down the Reach Lode and into the village of Reach. There is a 1-mile stretch on quiet roads after Reach.

3. The Village Explorer is a 19-mile route that loops through Swaffham Prior, Reach and Burwell; there are longer road sections on this route.

© ROSIE MAHER

Haddenham Horseshoe Ride 27

The fenland south of Ely is criss-crossed with byways and bridleways that offer excellent off-road riding on grassy tracks and gravel-topped trails. The suggested route is a horseshoe that begins north of the village of Haddenham (in Cambridgeshire, not to be confused with its Buckinghamshire namesake) and finishes to the east. With two village pubs, Haddenham is a great place to explore the fens from. If you're a keen mountain or gravel biker, it is well worth rolling out an Ordnance Survey map of the area and exploring the network of trails in this area.

On your bikes!

1. The route starts 3/4 mile north of Haddenham centre, on the A1421 by St George's Farm; there is a gate at the entrance to the byway, which may be locked. After 400m, turn right with the byway. After 600m, meet the New Cut Drain; turn left.

2. Follow the New Cut Drain for 2 miles to a road; cross the road and continue along the New Cut Drain for another 3/4 mile. At a track junction, turn right and continue to follow the New Cut Drain for 1.5 miles to emerge in the village of Aldreth.

3. Continue straight on, on the road for 400m, through the village; when the road turns sharply right, take the track on the left.

4. Continue straight on for 2 miles, crossing a road; at the second road, turn right then almost immediately left on to the bridleway. After 750m, turn right with the bridleway to reach the road on the outskirts of Wilburton.

5. The traffic-free route ends here, but it is possible to return to the start on quiet roads by turning left towards Wilburton (there is a shared-use cycle path next to the busy road). Turn right on to Station Road, and at the end of the road turn left on to Ely Way which reaches the A1421 near the start.

Refreshments: Three Kings and Cherry Tree pub in Haddenham, 1 mile from start. Red Lion in Stretham, 2 miles from end.
Bike hire and repairs: Bike shops in Ely.
Public transport and bike links: Ely train station, 6.5 miles from start and 6 miles from end, via quiet lanes, bridleways and byways.
Parking: Limited on-street parking in Haddenham and Wilburton.
Maps and guides: OS Landranger 143 & 154, Explorer 225 & 226.

Start
St George's Farm, Haddenham
(52.3691, 0.1511, TL 465767)

Finish
A1123, Wilburton
(52.3517, 0.1812, TL 487749)

Distance
9 miles/14.5km.

Category
Gravel-topped farm tracks, grassy trails.

Other facilities

139

Ride 28 Peterborough and Ferry Meadows Country Park

Start
Bridge by Rivergate Asda, Peterborough (52.5686, -0.2437, TL 191982)

Finish
Ferry Meadows Visitor Centre, Peterborough (52.5628, -0.3071, TL 148973)

Distance
7 miles/11.5km (optional 3-mile/5km loop of lakes).

Category
Tarmac cycle paths.

Other facilities

This traffic-free ride on either side of the River Nene between the centre of Peterborough and Ferry Meadows Country Park is part of a much larger and more ambitious project known as the Peterborough Green Wheel. This is a network of cycleways, footpaths and bridleways that provides safe, continuous routes around the city and 'spokes' linking the Wheel to residential areas and the city centre. The Green Wheel celebrates over 2,000 years of Peterborough's social, cultural, economic and environmental history through a series of sculptures and colourful interpretation boards along the route. For those who would prefer not to cycle back, the Nene Valley heritage railway runs between the finish and the start and carries bikes, space permitting. The ride described is just one suggestion; others might include a ride along the River Nene to the east of town or west from Farcet towards the A15 and A1.

On your bikes!

1. From the footbridge over the River Nene just south of the centre of Peterborough (near Asda), turn right on Henry Penn Walk alongside the river (keeping the water to your left).

2. At the T-junction at the end of the tarmac turn right to cross the bridge, then left by the Boathouse pub. Follow the path around the edge of the rowing lake, keeping the water to your left.

3. At the T-junction by the main road at the end of the lake, turn left, signposted 'Orton, Ferry Meadows'. Pass beneath the road bridge, over the green metal sluice gates, cross the railway line then turn right, signposted 'Orton Meadows, Ferry Meadows, Lynch Wood'.

4. At the next T-junction turn right to cross the railway line then turn left and stay close to the railway line. Cross the

Peterborough and Ferry Meadows Country Park — Ride 28

road with care, then turn right on the tarmac path alongside the road to the visitor centre at Ferry Meadows.

5. For a full circuit of the lakes, go past the visitor centre and at the first lake bear left, following the curve of the miniature railway line to your left. Pass to the left of the water sports centre then keep bearing right, staying on tarmac and keeping close to the lake to your right to return to the visitor centre.

6. To return to Peterborough along the south side of the River Nene, follow the tarmac path alongside the exit road from Ferry Meadows park then turn left just before the level crossing, signposted 'Station, Orton Mere, City Centre'.

7. Keep following the tarmac path as it crosses the railway line, then turn left, parallel with the line, signposted 'Orton Mere, City Centre'.

8. At the next junction, turn left then right, signposted 'Woodston City Centre' to continue parallel with railway line.

9. Stay on the tarmac path as it swings right then left to recross the railway line for a final time. Go past Railworld Wildlife Haven and take the next footbridge across the river (opposite yellow-brick riverside houses) to return to Asda.

Refreshments: Lots of choice in Peterborough. Boathouse pub, near to the rowing lake. Cafe at the Ferry Meadows Country Park.
Bike hire and repairs: Hire from Rutland Cycling, next to Ferry Meadows. Several bike shops in Peterborough, including Richardsons Cycles by the station.
Public transport and bike links: Peterborough station, $1/2$ mile from start; Nene Valley heritage railway connects start and finish (bikes carried); Peterborough station across river from start and Overton (for Ferry Meadows) station next to end.
Parking: Paid parking at Ferry Meadows; paid city car parks in Peterborough.
Maps and guides: OS Landranger 142, Explorer 227 & 235.
Website: *www.sustrans.org.uk/find-a-route-on-the-national-cycle-network/peterborough-green-wheel*

TRAFFIC-FREE CYCLE TRAILS SOUTH EAST ENGLAND

Eastern Counties

1 Thames at Tilbury
2 Southend-on-Sea
3 Hadleigh Country Park
4 Clacton-on-Sea to Frinton-on-Sea
5 Chelmer and Blackwater Navigation, Maldon
6 River Can in Chelmsford
7 Hatfield Forest
8 Flitch Way: Great Dunmow to Start Hill
9 Flitch Way: Braintree to Little Dunmow
10 Colchester to Wivenhoe
11 Grim's Dyke, Colchester
12 Alton Water
13 Trimley Marshes
14 Rendlesham Forest
15 Viking Trail
16 Valley Walk, Sudbury
17 Ickworth
18 Brandon Country Park
19 Thetford Forest
20 Little Ouse Path
21 The Bure Valley Path
22 Marriott's Way: Norwich to Reepham
23 Weavers' Way: Stalham to Bengate
24 Weavers' Way: Aylsham to North Walsham
25 Blickling Estate
26 Holkham Park
27 Peddars Way: Great Massingham to Fring
28 Sandringham Estate

Eastern Counties

05

Eastern Counties

CONTAINS ORDNANCE SURVEY DATA © CROWN COPYRIGHT AND DATABASE RIGHT

143

Ride 1 Thames at Tilbury

Start
Tilbury Town station, Tilbury
(51.4621, 0.3540, TQ 636163)

Finish
Coalhouse Fort, East Tilbury
(51.4649, 0.4321, TQ 690768)

Distance
4.5 miles/7.5km.

Category
Tarmac cycle paths, hard-surfaced trails.

Other facilities

National Cycle Network (NCN) Route 13 will eventually link London's Tower Bridge to Dereham in Norfolk, on a mixture of on-road and off-road sections. At Tilbury, you can enjoy a pleasant five-mile riverside section of the route that passes the historic Tilbury Fort, where Queen Elizabeth I disembarked to make her rallying speech to the troops, and continues along the edge of Tilbury marshes to reach Coalhouse Fort.

On your bikes!

1. With your back to the station, turn left on to the A1089 (signposted for the ferry terminal and Tilbury Fort); there is a shared-use footpath and cycleway. After ½ mile, the NCN 13 joins from the left.

2. After 200m cross at the toucan crossing, and after another 10m take the cycle path that forks to the right.

3. The cycle path runs parallel to the A1089, returning to run beside it after 500m, near a roundabout. Continue straight across the roundabout (on the shared-use path) to a second roundabout; you are now passing the ferry port and may encounter heavy traffic at road crossings.

Refreshments: Cafe and pubs in Tilbury, pub at Tilbury Fort.
Public transport and bike links: Tilbury station at start. Route is part of NCN 13.
Parking: Car parks in Tilbury and at Tilbury Fort.
Maps and guides: OS Landranger 177, Explorer 163.
Website: www.sustrans.org.uk/find-a-route-on-the-national-cycle-network/route-13

4. Follow the road round to the left, still on shared-used paths. After 200m, by the bus terminal, follow the cycle path as it forks away right from the road.

5. The trail continues for a further 3.5 miles along the riverbanks; it passes Tilbury Fort (and the Culloden memorial stone, placed to remember 45 Jacobite prisoners that died of typhus when they were imprisoned at the fort awaiting trial in London). The trail ends at Coalhouse Fort Park.

144

EASTERN COUNTIES

Southend-on-Sea Ride 2

A 4.5-mile section of the incomplete National Cycle Network (NCN) Route 16 offers a traffic-free seaside ride from Southend-on-Sea to Shoeburyness. The route is entirely on a segregated tarmac cycle path. The path is sometimes narrow and often on the edge of busy roads – it is also often poorly segregated from pedestrian paths.

On your bikes!

1. The trail begins at the junction of Chalkwell Avenue and Chalkwell Esplanade, as a segregated path by the road.

2. Follow the route for 4.5 miles on segregated tracks along the seafront to Shoeburyness.

Refreshments: Pubs and cafes in Southend.
Bike hire and repairs: Motion HUB bike-sharing stations on Southend seafront; Halfords 1 mile from start; several bike shops in Southend.
Public transport and bike links: Chalkwell station, 1/2 mile from start.
Parking: (Paid) on-street parking at start.
Maps and guides: OS Landranger 178, Explorer 176.
Website: *www.sustrans.org.uk/find-a-route-on-the-national-cycle-network/route-16*

Start
Junction of Chalkwell Avenue and Chalkwell Esplanade, Chalkwell
(51.5369, 0.6777, TQ 858854)

Finish
Mess Road, Shoeburyness
(51.5231, 0.7886, TQ 935842)

Distance
4.5 miles/7.5km.

Category
Tarmac cycle paths.

Other facilities

145

Ride 3 Hadleigh Country Park

Start/finish
The Hub, Hadleigh Country Park (51.5510, 0.5956, TQ 801868)

Distance
3 miles/5km or 5 miles/8km.

Category
Mountain bike tracks.

Other facilities

Hadleigh Country Park, situated between Canvey Island and Southend-on-Sea, is one of Essex's largest areas of greenspace and hosted mountain biking during the 2012 Olympics. The park has plenty to keep the family entertained, including a replica Iron Age roundhouse, water sports on the lake and a ruined castle. In addition to four different mountain bike trails, there is a skills area and a pump track to develop your riding. There is also a short purple route (less than a mile) that requires no experience, and is ideal for children.

On your bikes!
1. The green route is 5 miles in length and uses multi-use paths to explore the perimeter of the park, taking you past the ruined castle. It requires no technical skills and is family friendly. However, these paths may be busy with walkers, runners and occasionally cattle.

Refreshments: Cafe at start.
Bike hire and repairs: Hire, spares and repairs at Hadleigh Park Cycles, at start.
Public transport and bike links: Benfleet station, $1/2$ mile from south-west end of green route.
Parking: Paid parking at start.
Maps and guides: OS Landranger 178, Explorer 175.
Website: www.hadleighparkcycles.co.uk

2. A section of the forest is exclusively for mountain bike trails; there are three trails of approximately 3 miles. The blue trail is non-technical. The red trail requires a reasonable level of proficiency. The black trail is technically challenging and is a rare opportunity for expert riders to experience the thrills of an Olympic course.

EASTERN COUNTIES

Clacton-on-Sea to Frinton-on-Sea Ride 4

The National Cycle Network (NCN) Route 150 is a well-surfaced, traffic-free route between Clacton-on-Sea and Frinton-on-Sea that hugs the shore for 6.5 miles. There is a further traffic-free stretch to the north of Frinton, but you will need to negotiate the town's roads to reach this. The trail stops short of the centre of Frinton. It is well-segregated from roads and also from pedestrians, although you may find that walkers stray on to the path, particularly on Clacton's busy seafront.

On your bikes!
1. The route begins on the eastern fringes of Jaywick and follows the shore for 800m, passing a Martello tower, to reach the outskirts of Clacton.

2. Continue straight on, following the trail along the shoreline, for 4 miles through Clacton; you pass several more Martello towers and the pier.

3. Still on the seafront, follow the track for a further 1.5 miles through the country park.

4. The track continues on, traffic-free, for just over 1 mile, finishing near the public toilets.

Refreshments: Pubs and cafes in Clacton and Frinton.
Bike hire and repairs: Bike shops in Clacton and Frinton, for spares and repairs.
Public transport and bike links: Clacton-on-Sea station, 1/2 mile from trail/2 miles from start. Frinton-on-Sea station, 1 mile from finish.
Parking: Paid car parks in Jaywick. On-street parking in Frinton.
Maps and guides: OS Landranger 169, Explorer 184.
Website: *www.sustrans.org.uk/find-a-route-on-the-national-cycle-network/frinton-on-sea-to-clacton-on-sea*

Start
Jaywick Sands, Jaywick (51.7759, 1.1242, TM 156132)

Finish
Kiosk toilets, Frinton (51.8247, 1.2413, TM 235190)

Distance
6.5 miles/10.5km.

Category
Tarmac cycle paths.

Other facilities

© SHUTTERSTOCK/DAVID JOHN ABRAMS

Ride 5 Chelmer and Blackwater Navigation Maldon

Start
B1018, near Temple Way, Maldon (51.7404, 0.6753, TL 848080)

Finish
The lock at Heybridge Basin (51.7292, 0.7087, TL 872069)

Distance
2 miles/3km.

Category
Towpaths.

Other facilities

Both Maldon and Heybridge Basin are attractive destinations for summer visitors. At Maldon, you can stroll through the Promenade Park and see the Thames barges, or enjoy a boat trip. At Heybridge, you can take in sea views and visit the two pubs or tea rooms. The willow-fringed towpath along the Chelmer and Blackwater Navigation between Maldon and Heybridge Basin makes for an easy and pleasant two-mile ride along the waterfront. The trail is generally hard surfaced but there is a short section on a quiet road, and a narrower, muddier section. The trail is part of the National Cycle Network (NCN) Route 1, which is largely on-road.

On your bikes!

1. The route starts in the car park off the B1018 (opposite Temple Way). At the far end of the car park, turn left and follow the track. Turn left.

2. Just after passing under the A414 main road, turn left to follow the trail as it snakes through Oak Tree Meadow. Fork right just before the children's play area.

3. Follow the track along the banks of the Chelmer and Blackwater Navigation for 1/2 mile, passing under the A414 road again.

Refreshments: Pubs and cafe at end.
Bike hire and repairs: Spares and repairs at Riverside Cycle Centre, 3/4 mile from Oak Tree Meadow.
Public transport and bike links: Hatfield Peverel station, 5 miles from start. Part of NCN 1.
Parking: Free car park at start and finish.
Maps and guides: OS Landranger 168, Explorer 176.
Website: waterways.org.uk/waterways/discover-the-waterways/chelmer-blackwater-navigation

4. Pass under another road – there is an 80m section along a quiet road here. Where the road bends left, take the bridleway on the right to follow the narrow, muddy track along the Chelmer and Blackwater Navigation.

5. Continue to follow the trail along the Chelmer and Blackwater Navigation for 1.5 miles to reach Heybridge Basin; the trail soon improves from narrow, muddy singletrack to wider, well-surfaced bridleway.

148

EASTERN COUNTIES

River Can in Chelmsford Ride 6

National Cycle Network (NCN) Route 1 follows a traffic-free track beside the River Can as it passes through Chelmsford. The route is described here from the Essex Records Office on the banks of the River Chelmer, but the traffic-free section begins 1.5 miles east on Pollard's Green; much of this early section is shared-use pathway next to busy roads. The start of the route passes along shared-use paths by shops and cafes near the city centre. There is a 50-metre section along an access road, and you have to cross the river on New London Road — you either have to cycle on the busy road or push your bike across the bridge. However, you will soon find yourself rolling through the green parks that line the River Can. The trail ends at the Writtle University College campus, where NCN 1 rejoins roads. You can extend your ride if you cycle 1 mile south on quiet roads, through Writtle, to reach Hylands Park.

On your bikes!

1. From the Records Office, cross the river and turn right on to Kings Head Walk. Follow the busy shared-use path past shops and cafes for 500m.

2. Near Barrack Square, there is 50m of access road where you may encounter traffic. Continue for another 50m to reach New London Road; turn right to cross the bridge, either cycling on the busy road or dismounting to use the pavement.

3. Turn left into Bell Meadow Park and follow the track as it passes under the Parkway main road.

4. The track follows the riverbanks of the Can through Central Park and passes under A1016 main road into Admirals Park.

5. After 250m, cross the River Can and continue to follow the southern bank. After another 350m, by the bridge, turn left.

6. After 350m, at a junction of paths, turn right to cross the river. Turn left and then right to follow the trail to the bridge across the River Wid.

7. Turn left to cross the stream and then follow the trail for 250m to cross back to the southern banks of the River Can on the Lawford Lane footbridge.

8. Follow the trail across the university sports fields to finish at Writtle University College.

Refreshments: Pubs and cafes in Chelmsford.
Bike hire and repairs: Spares and repairs from bike shops in Chelmsford; closest, Chelmer Cycles, 1 mile from start.
Public transport and bike links: Chelmsford station, 1 mile from start.
Parking: Paid car park at start.
Maps and guides: OS Landranger 167, Explorer 183.

Start
Essex Records Office, Chelmsford
(51.7302 0.4803, TL 714064)

Finish
Writtle University College, Writtle
(51.7358, 0.4289, TL 678069)

Distance
3 miles/5km.

Category
Tarmac tracks.

Other facilities

149

Ride 7 **Hatfield Forest**

Start/finish
North Gate, Hatfield Forest (51.8688, 0.2257, TL 533213)

Distance
2 miles/3.5km.

Category
Mountain bike tracks.

Other facilities

Hatfield Forest is a National Trust estate criss-crossed with muddy tracks, perfect for mountain bikers (and adventurous gravel bikers). Cyclists are requested not to visit in the winter to avoid damage to trails, and trails may also be closed after wet weather. Almost all the tracks may be cycled, but the area immediately around the lake is out of bounds. It is a popular destination so expect to meet horse riders, trail runners and walkers on the tracks as well as other cyclists. There is a cafe (and toilets), should you want a hot drink after your adventure. The forest is just off the Flitch Way (between Great Dunmow and Start Hill – see the next ride).

Refreshments: Cafe at south-east end of Hatfield Forest.
Bike hire and repairs: None en route. Repairs at Blue Sky Bikes, Little Canfield. Several bike shops in Bishop's Stortford.
Public transport and bike links: Stansted Airport station, 3.5 miles from start. Flitch Way passes north of forest.
Parking: Paid parking at south-east end of Hatfield Forest.
Maps and guides: OS Landranger 167, Explorer 183 & 195.
Website: www.nationaltrust.org.uk/wimpole-estate/projects/wimpoles-multi-user-trail

On your bikes!

1. Enter the forest via the main North Gate at the north-western corner. After 500m, fork right to follow the waymarked Forest Way to the southern bottom of the forest.

2. Either follow the main trail back to the top or pick a zigzag route through the trails on the eastern side of the forest.

150

Flitch Way: Great Dunmow to Start Hill — Ride 8

The Flitch Way is a trail of two halves, both physically and in character. The eastern section, between Braintree and Little Dunmow (next ride), is generally a well-surfaced, broad trail that could be cycled by riders of any ability on any bikes. The western section, although not mountain bike territory, is a rougher, muddier proposition: it is often rutted and sometimes narrow or overgrown. Under good conditions, cautious riders might tackle it on any bike, but it is best suited to a gravel or hybrid. Both sections of the Flitch Way have narrow barriers and gates that might be problematic for non-standard bikes.

On your bikes!

1. The western section of the Way begins at the Dunmow Cutting, off the B1256 (approximately 400m south-east of the roundabout with Stortford Road).

2. Continue straight on along the Way, crossing under the A120 main road. At High Cross Lane East, you can either proceed through the Flitch Way car park or turn right on to the road, and turn left on to the Flitch Way after 80m.

Refreshments: Pubs and cafes in Great Dunmow, 1/2 mile from start.
Bike hire and repairs: Spares and repairs from Mike Barnard Cycles, Dunmow and Blue Sky Bikes Takeley.
Public transport and bike links: Stansted Airport station, 5 miles from finish.
Parking: On-street parking at start. Flitch Way car park at Little Canfield.
Maps and guides: OS Landranger 167, Explorer 195.
Website: *www.friends-of-the-flitch-way.org.uk*

3. Follow the Way for 3.5 miles to reach the disused Stane Street Halt; this shady, wooded section of the Way is often muddy and rutted as well as narrow, particularly as the Way is a shared-use trail.

4. The Way takes you past the northern edge of Hatfield Forest now, and there are several gates should you want to explore the National Trust estate. However, most are only suitable for mountain bikes — some are suitable for hybrid or gravel bikes under good conditions.

5. Continue on the Way for a little over 1 mile to reach Start Hill, where the Flitch Way ends; you can continue on for another 1.5 miles on the modern (2018) bridleway to reach Birchanger via Stansted Airport.

Start
Dunmow Cutting, Great Dunmow (51.8694, 0.3562, TL 623216)

Finish
Dunmow Road, Start Hill (51.8700, 0.2188, TL 529214)

Distance
6.5 miles/10.5km.

Category
Railway tracks.

Other facilities

© FRIENDS OF THE FLITCH WAY

Ride 9 Flitch Way: Braintree to Little Dunmow

Start
Car park, Braintree railway station (51.8751, 0.5544, TL 759227)

Finish
Near the A120, Little Dunmow (51.8614, 0.3867, TL 644208)

Distance
7.5 miles/12km.

Category
Railway tracks.

Other facilities

This wide railway path has been improved over the years and offers an easy, flat ride through the gently undulating Essex countryside. The trail starts conveniently from Braintree railway station car park, soon passing the handsome old buildings of Rayne station, which is now a tea room. A long footbridge over the new A120 takes you high above the traffic and back on to the wooded corridor leading westwards. There is one point (near the old Felsted station) where a bridge has been removed and you need to descend to the road before rejoining the path. Unfortunately the railway path does not continue into Great Dunmow, so you can either turn around at the end of the traffic-free section (perhaps visiting the pub in Little Dunmow or Maid Marian's grave at the village church) or negotiate the traffic of Great Dunmow to link with the western half of the Flitch Way. Both sections of the Flitch Way have narrow barriers and gates that might be problematic for non-standard bikes.

On your bikes!
1. Follow through the overflow car park (furthest from the railway station) to the start of the Flitch Way. The surface is at first tarmac.

Refreshments: Pubs in Little Dunmow, tea room at Rayne station.
Bike hire and repairs: Spares and repairs from Braintree Bike Repairs, Cycles UK, 1/2 mile from start.
Public transport and bike links: Braintree railway station, at start.
Parking: Station car park at start. On-street parking at Little Dunmow.
Maps and guides: OS Landranger 167, Explorer 195.
Website: www.friends-of-the-flitch-way.org.uk

2. Cross a bridge over a road then after 1.3 miles there is a chance of refreshments at the old station at Rayne. Shortly, cross a long bridge over the new A120.

3. After 3.3 miles and shortly after a 'Felsted Station' signpost, descend to the road, cross to the pavement opposite, turn right then left up a flight of steps. At the tarmac turn left then right on to a continuation of the railway path, passing above a travellers' site. If you wish to visit the Flitch of Bacon pub at Little Dunmow, immediately after passing under the next bridge turn right, then at the lane turn left and follow this road (Brook Road) into Little Dunmow, turning left at the T-junction for the pub.

4. The railway path ends after a further 1.5 miles where 'National Cycle Network Route 16' is signposted off to the right. You can continue into Great Dunmow following National Cycle Network (NCN) Route 16 signs, although this will involve using busier roads; work has begun on the construction of a traffic-free route, for pedestrians and cyclists, to link the two halves of the Flitch Way and avoid the roads.

EASTERN COUNTIES

Colchester to Wivenhoe Ride 10

This ride links Colchester to Wivenhoe Quay via a mixture of quiet streets, paths through parkland and (for the greater part of the ride) a traffic-free riverside path along the River Colne from the south-eastern edge of Colchester past the University of Essex to Wivenhoe railway station. It is well worth going beyond the station to explore the quay and pubs by the riverside in Wivenhoe. For those of you looking for a totally traffic-free ride, it would be best to start at Wivenhoe station and turn around at the end of the cycle path after three miles. However, if you are prepared to use some short sections on quiet streets you soon join another traffic-free stretch alongside the river and through parkland, arriving right in the heart of Colchester's historic city centre.

On your bikes!

1. Start at the Tenpin bowling car park. Follow the tarmac cycle path (white line down the middle) directly away from the Tenpin bowling, soon passing a 'Wivenhoe Trail' sign. Cross a bridge and turn left, keeping close to the water on your left and following 'Wivenhoe Trail' signs through the parkland.

2. Cross the busy road via a toucan crossing. Pass between allotments and past metal sculptures. Briefly join a road. Cross a bridge and turn left on to Hawkins Road through the industrial estate.

3. Immediately before the roundabout cross the road to join a cycle path. Use the toucan crossing to cross this very busy road.

4. Follow the riverside path for 3 miles, passing the University of Essex up to your left. The trail passes through woodland with the railway to your left and the river to your right, and emerges at Wivenhoe station.

5. It is worth exploring the riverfront along Old Ferry Road, maybe taking refreshments in Wivenhoe.

Refreshments: Pubs and cafes in Wivenhoe. Lots of choice in Colchester.
Bike hire and repairs: Several bike shops in Colchester; Halfords opposite side of Cowdray Avenue at start; Route 51 Cycle Project offers mobile repair.
Public transport and bike links: Colchester station, $3/4$ mile from start; route also passes Hythe station near start. Finishes at Wivenhoe station. Route is part of National Cycle Network (NCN) Route 51 (between Oxford and Colchester); Colchester is on NCN 1.
Parking: Paid parking at start and finish.
Maps and guides: OS Landranger 168, Explorer 184.

Start
Tenpin bowling, Colchester (51.8970, 0.9045, TL 999260)

Finish
Wivenhoe station, Wivenhoe (51.8564, 0.9562, TM 037217)

Distance
5 miles/8km.

Category
Riverside paths, tarmac cycle paths.

Other facilities

Ride 11 Grim's Dyke Colchester

Start/finish
Heath Road/
Stanway Green,
Colchester
(51.8741, 0.8459,
TL 960233)

Distance
6 miles/10km.

Category
Hard-surfaced
trails, tarmac
lanes, grassy farm
tracks.

Other facilities

Colchester has great cycling infrastructure (and more is being constructed) but this loop takes advantage of bridleways to escape the town and explore its green surrounds. The loop offers plenty to distract you, passing historic sites and Colchester Zoo. The trail is generally on hard-surfaced tracks, but south of Colchester Zoo it follows grassy bridleways that may be muddy. However, there are plenty of route options to avoid muddy sections and also a short section along a quiet road.

On your bikes!

1. Take the bridleway (signposted as a footpath) that forks right off Heath Road, if coming from Fiveways. The bridleway follows the course of the Iron Age Grim's Dyke earthworks for nearly 1 mile.

2. At the often-busy Maldon Road, turn right on the road for 500m if you wish to detour to the zoo; there is alternative footpath access further on down the bridleway. Continue on the bridleway for 400m to the south-west corner of Butcher's Wood, then dismount and follow the footpath right for traffic-free access to the zoo.

3. If you're not detouring to the zoo, turn left then immediately right to continue straight on. This is where the bridleway may become muddy; to avoid muddy sections, do not make the immediate right turn but instead continue straight on along the edge of Butcher's Wood.

4. After 1/2 mile, the bridleway turns to the left. Continue on the bridleway, ignoring two other bridleways that join from the right for another 1/2 mile; near Hill Farm, the trail becomes hard-surfaced farm lanes.

5. Turn left with the bridleway; after 1/2 mile you will reach some houses. There is a 250m stretch along a quiet country

Grim's Dyke, Colchester — Ride 11

road here. The road can be avoided by turning left on to the bridleway. When you reach the south-east corner of Butcher's Wood, turn right to follow the bridleway up the edge of the wood. After 1 mile, reach Cheshunt Field to rejoin the main route at step 7.

6. If you are happy to continue on the road, take the bridleway to the left after 250m. The entrance is a narrow gap in the hedgerow that is often overgrown, so it is easily missed. After 250m, the bridleway turns right – follow it for almost 1 mile.

7. At a track junction near the ancient settlement site of Cheshunt Field, turn right (or left if coming from Butcher's Wood) to follow the bridleway to Cheshunt Field car park.

Refreshments: Cafes and pubs, Colchester (within 1 mile of start).
Bike hire and repairs: Spares and repairs at Cycle Revolution, $1/2$ mile from start.
Public transport and bike links: Marks Tey station, 3.5 miles from start; Colchester Town station, 4 miles from start; Colchester has good network of cycle paths.
Parking: On-street parking at start.
Maps and guides: OS Landranger 168, Explorer 184.

8. Cross the Maldon Road again and follow the well-surfaced bridleway along the edge of Westlands Country Park; turn left on Stanway Green road to return to the start.

Ride 12 Alton Water

Start/finish
Alton Water Visitor Centre, Stutton (51.9745, 1.1381, TM 156353)

Distance
3 miles/5km to 15 miles/24km.

Category
Forestry trails, mixed-surface trails.

Other facilities

This fine reservoir circuit is being improved a little more each year, making the route safer and easier with each improvement. Alton Water is also popular with water sports, so on fine, breezy days you will catch sight of windsurfers racing each other across the lake with their bright sails skimming over the surface. Although this is a relatively easy and flat ride, you should be warned that there is a (short) hillier and rougher stretch on the north side of the lake between Birchwood car park and Lemons Bay. A map showing the route plus the surrounding lanes is available from the cycle hire centre. There is a cafe at the visitor centre and several pubs just near the route, so you could either follow the circuit close to the lake itself or make this part of a longer ride, exploring some of the beautiful and quiet lanes on the Shotley Peninsula.

On your bikes!

1. From the visitor centre keep the water to your right and follow the numbered waymarkers for the Alton Water Circuit clockwise around the lake.

2. After 3 miles, at the road, turn right over the bridge then right again through the car park on to a gravel track, following the bike route signposts. Certain sections on the north side of the lake are a bit rough and there are some steeper climbs and descents.

3. Cross the dam and follow the lake shore round to the right, back to the start.

Refreshments: Cafe at start. Pubs in Tattingstone, Stutton and Holbrook.
Bike hire and repairs: Alton Cycle Hire (located in water sports centre, near start). Closest bike shops in Manningtree (5 miles away).
Public transport and bike links: Buses from Ipswich to Manningtree stop every 2 hours at park entrance. Manningtree station, 5.5 miles away.
Parking: Paid car park at start.
Maps and guides: OS Landranger 169, Explorer 197; map available from website (below).
Website: anglianwaterparks.co.uk/alton-water

EASTERN COUNTIES

Trimley Marshes Ride 13

Trimley Marshes is a remote nature reserve near Felixstowe. These, however, are not historic wetlands: they were created out of farmland to compensate for the loss of mudflats when the port of Felixstowe expanded in the 1990s. The route is generally hard-surfaced bridleway but is often narrow and may be muddy in wet conditions. The land is owned by Trinity College Cambridge (as is the neighbouring port of Felixstowe).

On your bikes!

1. At the end of Thorpe Lane, turn right and, after the houses, turn left on to the bridleway. The trail is tarmac for 300m and then becomes hard surfaced; after $^1/_2$ mile, reach the banks of the River Orwell.

2. Follow the bridleway along the edge of the River Orwell for 2 miles to reach the edge of the port of Felixstowe. Take the bridleway around the edge of the port for 1.5 miles.

3. Turn left to follow the bridleway as it runs beside the railway for nearly 1 mile, and then turn left to reach Trimley St Mary.

Refreshments: Pub, Trimley St Martin, $^1/_2$ mile from start. Fish and chip shop, $^1/_2$ mile from finish.
Bike hire and repairs: Nearest bike shops in Felixstowe, 2 miles from end.
Public transport and bike links: Trimley station, 400m from end.
Parking: Free car park at end. On-street parking in Trimley St Martin.
Maps and guides: OS Landranger 169, Explorer 197.
Website: *www.suffolkwildlifetrust.org/trimleymarshes*

Start
Thorpe Lane, Trimley St Martin (51.9915, 1.2963, TM 264377)

Finish
Cordy's Lane, Trimley St Mary (51.9744, 1.3158, TM 278358)

Distance
3 miles/5km.

Category
Sandy trails, hard-surfaced tracks, tarmac lanes.

Other facilities

© SHUTTERSTOCK/ROB ATHERTON

157

Ride 14 **Rendlesham Forest**

Start/finish
Rendlesham Forest Centre (52.0841, 1.4337, TM 354484)

Distance
3 miles/5km to 15 miles/24km.

Category
Forestry trails, mixed-surface trails.

Other facilities

There are two family cycle trails starting from Rendlesham Forest Centre as well as a skills area. The short trail, waymarked yellow (the Tang trail), is approximately six miles long with a shortcut allowing you to halve your ride. The long trail, waymarked green (the F.I.D.O trail), is 10 miles in length. Both trails are off-road on sand, gravel and grass. The rides pass through mixed woodland and clumps of bright-yellow gorse. The loops intersect, so it is possible to connect them to make a 15-mile circuit. Rendlesham Forest was planted by the Forestry Commission between 1922 and the late 1930s. Before that the land was heathland. Two-thirds of the forest was prematurely felled by the Great Storm of 1987, when over 1 million trees were blown down. The forest has since been redesigned to take account of wildlife conservation, recreation and timber production. It now has greater diversity, with conifer and broadleaf woodland, open space, wetland and heathland. It lies within the Suffolk Coast and Heaths Area of Outstanding Natural Beauty.

On your bikes!

1. The F.I.D.O (Fog Investigation and Dispersal Operation) trail is a waymarked, 10-mile, figure-of-eight loop that circles the central and northern areas of the forest. It follows the southern, eastern and northern perimeters of the airfield for much of its route.

2. The Tang trail is a 6-mile waymarked trail that follows the southern perimeter of the airfield and loops around the southern half of the forest. There is a white-waymarked shortcut back to the start that allows you to shorten the route to 3 miles.

Refreshments: Pub at Butley, 2 miles from start.
Bike hire and repairs: Spares and repairs from Hasnip's, Woodbridge, 7 miles from start.
Public transport and bike links: Melton station, 5.5 miles from start.
Parking: Paid car park at start.
Maps and guides: OS Landranger 156 & 169, Explorer 197 & 212; trail maps available from Forest Centre.
Website: *www.forestryengland.uk/rendlesham-forest*

EASTERN COUNTIES

Viking Trail Ride 15

Tunstall Forest is a Forestry-UK-managed broadleaf and conifer woodland in the Suffolk Coast and Heaths Area of Outstanding Natural Beauty, near Sutton Hoo. It is a popular spot for walkers and for birdwatchers, but there is also a 10-mile-long mountain biking trail through the forest. The trail began because of motorcycle enduro events in the forest. It is a red-grade trail, so suitable for proficient mountain bikers and not beginners. The trail is well waymarked, but is often narrow singletrack.

Refreshments: Pubs at Blaxhall and Tunstall, 1.5 miles from start.
Public transport and bike links: Wickham Market station, 4 miles from start.
Parking: Free car park at start.
Maps and guides: OS Landranger 156 & 169, Explorer 212.
Website: *www.forestryengland.uk/tunstall-forest/viking-trail-tunstall-forest*

Start/finish
Tunstall Forest car park, off Tunstall Road (52.1504, 1.4781, TM 380559)

Distance
10 miles/16km.

Category
Mountain bike trails.

Other facilities

On your bikes!

1. The trail begins at the car park in the north-west corner of the forest, just off Tunstall Road. It heads south then east on well-surfaced forestry tracks.

2. After $1/2$ mile, the trail leaves the forestry tracks behind and heads towards the western edge of the forest.

3. After a little over 1 mile following the western edge the trail wiggles east, and after just over 1 mile, takes a near loop around the south-eastern corner of the forest.

4. At about 6 miles from the start, you can choose a shortcut by following the forestry track north-west back to the car park. Alternatively, follow the trail along the eastern edge of the forest, close to Snape Road.

5. After nearly 3 miles the trail turns west and then south to rejoin forestry tracks back to the car park.

159

Ride 16 Valley Walk Sudbury

Start
Kingfisher Leisure Centre, Sudbury (52.0354, 0.7332, TL 876410)

Finish
Rod Bridge, Brundon (52.0597, 0.7063, TL 856410)

Distance
3 miles/5km.

Category
Railway tracks.

Other facilities

One of few dismantled railways in Suffolk that has been converted to recreational use, this follows the delightful River Stour which forms the boundary between Suffolk and Essex for much of its length. The trail can be linked to a picnic site by the River Stour to the south-west of Rodbridge Corner by crossing the road bridge at the end of the trail to the other bank of the river. You might also choose to head east along the network of quiet Essex/Suffolk lanes to the village pubs in Belchamp Otten, Belchamp St Paul and Pentlow.

On your bikes!

1. With your back to the leisure centre entrance, the start of the path is to your right in the corner of the car park. Follow it for 700m, crossing a tributary of the River Stour; reach a bridge to cross to the opposite side of the River Stour.

2. After a further 250m, the Stour Valley Path forks left but the Valley Walk continues straight on, following the path of the railway.

Refreshments: Lots of choice in Sudbury. Tea rooms and micropub at Rodbridge Corner, 500m from end.
Bike hire and repairs: Spares and repairs from Torque Bikes, Sudbury, $1/2$ mile from start.
Public transport and bike links: Start adjacent to Sudbury station. Valley Walk is part of the (incomplete and largely on-road) National Cycle Network (NCN) Route 13 from London to Dereham.
Parking: Paid parking at Kingfisher Leisure Centre car park at Long Melford Country Park, 250m from end.
Maps and guides: OS Landranger 155, Explorer 196.

3. Follow the railway for a further 2 miles to reach Rod Bridge.

EASTERN COUNTIES

Ickworth Ride 17

Ickworth was the ancestral home of the aristocratic Hervey family from 1432 to 1999; the spectacular Italianate-style mansion, with its striking rotunda, dates from the early 1800s. The new owners, the National Trust, constructed a six-mile, multi-use trail around the estate grounds in 2020; there is a shorter three-mile trail along the River Linnet. The accessible trail is suitable for wheelchairs and prams as well as all types of bike, although there are several gates to negotiate. There is a charge to enter this National Trust estate.

On your bikes!

1. From the visitor centre, turn right towards the lodge and continue on to reach the River Linnet after 1 mile.

2. Cross the river and turn left, to follow the trail for 1.25 miles.

3. At a second bridge, do not cross the river but turn right through the woods for 3 miles, passing the monument.

4. Cross the river again and turn left; after $1/2$ mile, by the walled garden, turn right to return to the visitor centre.

Refreshments: Cafe at start and at Ickworth House.
Bike hire and repairs: Bikes available to hire for guests at Ickworth Hotel (on estate); bike shops in Bury St Edmunds, 3 miles from start.
Public transport and bike links: Bury St Edmunds station, 4 miles from start.
Parking: Free parking at start (charge to enter estate).
Maps and guides: OS Landranger 155, Explorer 210 & 211; estate map on National Trust website.
Website: *www.nationaltrust.org.uk/ickworth*

Start/finish
Ickworth Estate Visitor Centre, Horringer (52.222, 0.6563, TL 815615)

Distance
6 miles/9.5km.

Category
Estate roads, hard-surfaced trails.

Other facilities

© SHUTTERSTOCK/RAEDWALD

161

Ride 18 Brandon Country Park

Start
Visitor Centre, Brandon Country Park (52.4363, 0.6252, TL 785853)

Finish
Visitor Centre, West Stow Country Park (52.3113, 0.6381, TL 799714)

Distance
14 miles/23km.

Category
Gravel tracks, tarmac, sandy trails.

Other facilities

Brandon Country Park was the country estate of Edward Bliss, a local businessman who made his fortune selling flint during the Napoleonic Wars. The pleasant, wooded landscape on the edge of Thetford Forest is now a popular destination for walkers and cyclists. The trail described here is the Brecks Trail which links Brandon Country Park to West Stow Country Park, although you could choose instead to follow the blue-waymarked Poacher Trail that loops around the country park.

Refreshments: Cafes at start and finish.
Bike hire and repairs: Bike Art (hire, spares and repairs) at Bike Art, High Lodge, 2 miles from start. Hire also available to Center Parcs guests at Elveden Forest.
Public transport and bike links: Brandon station, 1.5 miles from start.
Parking: Paid parking at start and finish.
Maps and guides: OS Landranger 143 & 144, Explorer 229.
Website: www.westsuffolk.gov.uk/leisure/Parks/brandoncountrypark.cfm

On your bikes!

1. From the visitor centre in Brandon Country Park, follow the blue cycle route through the car park, next to the playground, and past the care home. Continue straight on, on the blue route, as it heads south through the park.

2. After ½ mile, turn right with the blue route along Shakers Road. Do not turn right again with the blue route but continue straight on for a further 1.5 miles to reach the edge of the forest.

3. Continue straight on for a further 1 mile to Mossy Bottom, where the trail kinks right then almost immediately left.

4. Continue straight on for 1 mile and turn left along the Partition Belt. After 1 mile turn right to cross under London Road by the Elveden War Memorial.

5. Continue straight on to join the Duke's Track. After 2 miles, you reach the B1106. Either turn right on to the road for 600m and then turn right on to the Icknield Way, or if you prefer to avoid the road you can cross the road and continue on, turning right at Barrow's Corner after 450 metres, to join the Icknield Way; continue on for 600m to recross the B1106.

6. Follow the Icknield Way for 4 miles. If you want to reach the West Stow Country Park Visitor Centre (with its toilets and cafe), you will have to turn left on to the road and right at the park entrance after 800m.

© LIZ CUTHBERTSON

EASTERN COUNTIES

Thetford Forest Ride 19

Draw a line 10 miles around Thetford and you have some of the most consistently rideable off-road tracks in all of East Anglia: the soil has a sandy base and drains well and as the land is not good enough for farming, most of it is owned by Forestry England and planted with pine trees. The forestry tracks around the plantations tend to have excellent all-year-round surfaces and it is possible to devise any number of loops using these tracks. However, as is the case with all forestry land, it is almost impossible to give detailed route instructions when the only landmarks are trees and more trees, so the rides described are those that Forestry England has already waymarked.

On your bikes!
1. The Shepherd Trail is 5 miles long (although it has a shortcut) and is appropriate for beginners. It is suitable for most bike types.

2. The Beater Trail is 6 or 11 miles long (depending on whether you pick the short or long loop) and is a singletrack off-road route suitable for mountain or gravel bikers with a bit of experience.

3. The Lime Burner Trail is 10 miles long and is a singletrack route suitable for experienced mountain bikers only.

Refreshments: Cafe at High Lodge.
Bike hire and repairs: Bike Art (hire, spares and repairs) at High Lodge.
Public transport and bike links: Railway stations at Brandon (4 miles away) and Thetford (5 miles away). Thetford Forest, poorly served by bus; services between Brandon and Thetford stop at Thetford Gate every $1/2$ hour.
Parking: Paid parking at High Lodge.
Maps and guides: OS Landranger 143 & 144, Explorer 229.
Website: *www.forestryengland.uk/thetford-forest*

Start/finish
High Lodge Forest Centre, Thetford (52.4347, 0.6626, TL 811852)

Distance
5 miles/8km (Shepherd Trail, green grade, easy); 6 or 11 miles/10 or 18km (Beater Trail, blue grade, moderate); 10 miles/16km (Lime Burner Trail, red grade, difficult).

Category
Forest trails.

Other facilities

NB *If you decide to link rides either side of the B1106, take great care at the crossing points as traffic travels fast along this road.*

163

Ride 20 Little Ouse Path

Start
Bridge over Little Ouse, Santon Downham (52.4584, 0.674, TL 818879)

Finish
Riverside Way, Brandon (52.4518, 0.6238, TL 784870)

Distance
3 miles/5km.

Category
Hard-surfaced tracks, grassy tracks.

Other facilities

There were once plans to link Thetford to Brandon, with a cycle path that would take advantage of existing towpaths and bridges, but the plans were never realised. However, it is still possible to cycle sections of towpath, such as the Little Ouse Path between Santon Downham and Brandon. The path is often hard surfaced, but the tracks are sometimes grassy; access to the path from Santon Downham is via shallow steps and a narrow entrance, an obvious indication that the trail is not a good choice for non-standard bikes.

On your bikes!

1. From the distinctive white bridge, take the steps down to the north banks of the river.

2. Follow the towpath for nearly 3 miles to reach Brandon, emerging on the

Refreshments: The Ram Inn in Brandon, adjacent to finish.
Bike hire and repairs: Bike Art (hire, spares and repairs) at Bike Art, High Lodge, 3 miles from start.
Public transport and bike links: Brandon station, $^1/_2$ mile from finish.
Parking: Limited on-street parking in Santon Downham. On-street parking in Brandon.
Maps and guides: OS Landranger 144, Explorer 229.

Riverside Way. You can continue on the bridleway for another 4 miles to Hockwold cum Wilton, but you will encounter short sections of footpath where you will have to dismount.

© JOE JACKSON

164

EASTERN COUNTIES

The Bure Valley Path Ride 21

Steam trains chug along the heritage Bure Valley Railway for nine miles between Aylsham and Wroxham; a cycle and walking trail runs next to the line for its entire length. The compacted track is ungenerous in width at points, and is somewhat rutted and potholed occasionally. As the route is shared with pedestrians, this bluebell- and wild-garlic-fringed track is better explored in spring than in the busier summer days. Because of the narrow track and gates en route, this is not an accessible choice for non-standard bikes. Space permitting, bikes are carried on the heritage railway for a small fee.

On your bikes!
1. The path starts to the side of the ticket office at Wroxham station. Follow the track on the southern/western side of the railway for 2.5 miles; take care at the road crossing on Belaugh Lane.

2. Coltishall, nicknamed 'the Gateway to the Broads', has several pubs and cafes as well as a bike hire shop. Continue on the south side of the tracks for a further 2 miles, and at Hautbois Hall cross the railway track via a gated level crossing. Continue on to Buxton station; the village has a pub and fish and chip shop.

3. On the northern side of the tracks, continue on for 1.5 miles to Brampton and then a further $3/4$ mile to a road crossing; there are kissing gates to negotiate here.

4. After $3/4$ mile, you have to cross the often-busy A140 main road; the crossing is protected by gates. The railway passes under the road by tunnel; rejoin the tracks for a further 600m to reach Aylsham station; the track emerges into the station car park via a narrow-fenced path behind houses.

Refreshments: Whistlestop Cafe at Aylsham station. Pubs and cafes in Aylsham, Coltishall, Buxton and Wroxham.
Bike hire and repairs: Spares, repairs and hire at Aylsham Cycle Centre, 500m from Aylsham station. Hire from Bure Valley Cycle Hire, Coltishall station. Hire and repairs at Broadland Cycle Hire at Bewilderwood, 2 miles from Wroxham station.
Public transport and bike links: Start adjacent to Hoveton and Wroxham station. Bure Valley Railway carries bikes, space permitting.
Parking: Wroxham and Aylsham station car parks.
Maps and guides: OS Landranger 134, Explorer OL40 & 238.
Website: *www.bvrw.co.uk/activities/cycling*

Start
Hoveton and Wroxham station, Wroxham (52.7169, 1.4082, TG 303187)

Finish
Aylsham station, Aylsham (52.7912, 1.2559, TG 196265)

Distance
9 miles/15km.

Category
Compacted tracks.

Other facilities

© CHRIS COLES

165

Ride 22 Marriott's Way: Norwich to Reepham

Start
Roundabout at junction of Barn Road and St Crispins Road, by River Wensum, Norwich (52.6357, 1.2873, TG 225093)

Finish
1 mile south of crossroads in Reepham centre, at old Whitwell and Reepham station, Reepham (52.7525, 1.0975, TG 091217)

Distance
15 miles/24km.

Category
Railway tracks.

Other facilities

Escape from the heart of Norwich into the countryside on one of the longest disused railways in the country. The route is signposted as the 'Wensum Valley Walk' from the centre of Norwich, and becomes the Marriott's Way near to Drayton. If you do not live in Norwich itself, Reepham is a better place to start. The woodlands of Mileplain Plantation are a real delight: a deep cutting planted with sweet chestnut trees, especially attractive during the changing autumn colours. The whole route is studded with a wide variety of broadleaf trees: oak, ash, hawthorn, silver birch and sycamore. The clear, gently flowing waters of the River Wensum are crossed three times on fine old metal bridges with wooden planking. Between Lenwade and Reepham you have the option of the full route following the Themelthorpe Loop, or taking a shortcut that saves four miles.

On your bikes!

1. From the Barn Road/St Crispins Road roundabout in the centre of Norwich, join the track alongside the river, signposted 'Wensum Valley Walk'.

2. Follow 'National Cycle Network (NCN) Route 1' signs along a tarmac then gravel path for 5 miles, crossing one road and continuing in the same direction (take either fork after the road crossing – they join up).

3. Shortly after a triangular-shaped metal bridge over the river, the railway path peters out. Descend to the left then, at the T-junction with the road, turn right then left on to Station Road, signposted 'No through traffic'. At the T-junction at the end of Station Road, turn right then left through a gap in the wooden fence signposted 'Marriott's Way' to descend to a continuation of the railway paths.

Marriott's Way: Norwich to Reepham — Ride 22

4. Over the next 4 miles go straight ahead at several crossroads, following signs for Reepham.

5. At the T-junction with the road, turn right, signposted 'Reepham', then after 150 metres turn left on a broad gravel track. Go through the car park to rejoin the course of the railway.

6. Cross the river. The industrial estate begins to the left. Go straight ahead at several crossroads.

7. About 3 miles after passing the industrial estate and immediately after passing the old Whitwell and Reepham station, turn right*. You may wish to turn around here, or if you want refreshments in Reepham follow the minor road uphill and past the school to the crossroads in the centre of the town.

* Or continue straight ahead on the Themelthorpe Loop on a much longer (traffic-free) course into Reepham.

Refreshments: Lots of choice in Reepham and Norwich, and just off-route in Drayton and Lenwade.

Bike hire and repairs: Beryl Bikes share scheme in Norwich – bikes must be returned to a parking bay in the city. Several cycle shops in Norwich; spares and repairs at Reepham Cycle Workshop, on Marriott's Way leaving Reepham.

Public transport and bike links: Norwich station, 1.5 miles from start. Marriott's Way is part of NCN 1, on- and off-road cycle trail linking Dover to Scotland.

Parking: Westwick Street and Barn Street (paid) car parks near Norwich start.

Maps and guides: OS Landranger 133 & 134, Explorer 237 & 238.

Website: *www.marriottsway.info*

NB *The railway path can be followed east (for a further 11 miles) from Reepham to Aylsham where it is possible to link to the Bure Valley Path and Weavers' Way (p169) or explore the Blickling Estate (p170). However, the surface is much rougher and the shared-use track is narrow; there is often narrow gated access at road-crossing points.*

Ride 23 Weavers' Way: Stalham to Bengate

Start
High Street, near junction with A149, Stalham (52.7726, 1.5096, TG 368252)

Finish
A149, Bengate (52.7956, 1.4195, TG 306195)

Distance
5 miles/8km.

Category
Disused railway, compacted tracks.

Other facilities

The Weavers' Way is a 62-mile trail that generally follows the path of the disused railway bed between Aylsham and Great Yarmouth. Most of it can be cycled; the section between Aylsham and North Walsham is also described (next ride). Between Stalham and Bengate, the trail is occasionally stone-tracked but is often a muddy singletrack through woods. It is ideally suited to a gravel or hybrid bike. Single-width gates at road crossings make it difficult to navigate on a non-standard bike.

On your bikes!

1. Join the Weavers' Way from Stalham's High Street, at the site of the old railway station, near the junction with the A149. Follow it north for 2 miles, crossing Stepping Stone Lane after 600m.

2. Near East Ruston, the Way turns west to meander beside the North Walsham and Dilham Canal; follow it for a further 3 miles.

Refreshments: Cafes and pubs in Stalham. Pub in East Ruston, $^1/_2$ mile north of route.
Public transport and bike links: Worstead station, 2.5 miles from Bengate. Hourly direct bus service between Bengate and Stalham.
Parking: On-street parking and car parks in Stalham. Weavers' Way car park in East Ruston.
Maps and guides: OS Landranger 133, Explorer 252 or Explorer OL40.
Website: www.norfolk.gov.uk/out-and-about-in-norfolk/norfolk-trails/cycle-routes/weavers-way

© CHRIS COLES

EASTERN COUNTIES

Weavers' Way: Aylsham to North Walsham
Ride 24

The 62-mile Weavers' Way generally follows the disused railway bed between Aylsham and Great Yarmouth. Most of it can be cycled, although the track is sometimes poorly surfaced and muddy, and often narrow singletrack; a gravel or hybrid bike is ideally suited to the Way. The section described here goes from Drabblegate, just north of Aylsham, to North Walsham; it is easily joined to the Blickling Estate (p170), Bure Valley Path (p165) or Marriott's Way (p166) trails. It does begin with an 800-metre section along a country lane, however this is not a through road, so you will generally only encounter farm and access traffic. There are single-width gates at some of the road crossings, making it difficult to access on a non-standard bike.

Refreshments: Cafes and pubs in Aylsham and North Walsham.
Bike hire and repairs: Spares, repairs and hire at Aylsham Cycle Centre, 500m from Aylsham station. Spares and repairs from Doctor Wheelgood, North Walsham, 700m from end.
Public transport and bike links: North Walsham station, 600m from trail end. Heritage Bure Valley railway in Aylsham, 1 mile from start.
Parking: Limited on-street parking on residential roads near Drabblegate. Car park at trail end in North Walsham.
Maps and guides: OS Landranger 133, Explorer 252.
Website: www.norfolk.gov.uk/out-and-about-in-norfolk/norfolk-trails/cycle-routes/weavers-way

Start
Drabblegate, Aylsham (52.8030, 1.2611, TG 199278)

Finish
Weavers' Way car park, North Walsham (52.8197, 1.375, TG 275300)

Distance
6 miles/9km.

Category
Disused railway, compacted tracks.

Other facilities

On your bikes!

1. From the road junction, take the right-hand fork of Banningham Road and follow it for 800m. Turn right on to the grassy track which cuts across the road by a 'No Through Road' sign.

2. After 250m, take care when crossing the busy A140 main road.

3. Continue to follow the Weavers' Way for 4.5 miles, crossing two minor roads (and passing on bridges over two more) to reach the Weavers' Way car park in North Walsham.

© SHEREE HOOKER, WINGING THE WORLD

169

Ride 25 Blickling Estate

Start/finish
Muddy Boots Cafe, Blickling Estate (52.8107, 1.2277, TG 176286)

Distance
4 miles/6.5km.

Category
Gravel tracks.

Other facilities

Blickling Hall is a seventeenth-century stately home now owned by the National Trust, and it is set in a pleasant estate of woods and parkland. The National Trust constructed a multi-use, all-weather, carrstone-topped trail around the edge of the estate in 2017; it is designed for cyclists of all abilities and all types of bike. The trail is only open when the estate is open to visitors (which in winter may only be between 10 a.m. and 3 p.m.) and may be closed for events.

On your bikes!

1. The multi-use track around the perimeter of the estate has green waymarking; it begins at the rear of the car park near the visitor information. After 125m, take the left fork and turn left after another 125m.

2. 200m past the tower, now luxury holiday accommodation, stay straight on at the path junction. Continue on through Hyde Park and the Great Wood.

3. At the junction near the mausoleum, turn left. After 700m, turn right to return to the start; you can instead continue straight on to visit the lake and extend your route slightly.

Refreshments: Cafe at start; pub adjacent to start.
Bike hire and repairs: Bike hire at start. Hire, spares and repairs at Aylsham Cycle Centre, 1.5 miles from start.
Public transport and bike links: Blickling Estate is served by 1 daily school bus. Heritage Bure Valley railway in Aylsham, 2 miles from start. North Walsham station, 7.5 miles from start. Weavers' Way, which passes through estate, provides largely traffic-free route.
Parking: Paid parking at start.
Maps and guides: OS Landranger 133, Explorer 238.
Website: www.nationaltrust.org.uk/blickling-estate

© WWW.CHIMPTRIPS.COM

Holkham Park Ride 26

The Palladian Holkham Hall is the seat of the Earls of Leicester; the grounds and hall were designed for Thomas Coke, first Earl of Leicester, by William Kent in the early eighteenth century. The manicured grassy lawns and leafy copses offer flat, shaded routes along tarmac roads and gravel-topped paths. The tracks around the lake are grassy and may be muddy, but are easily omitted. There are several more miles of track in the park to explore, some offering muddy or tree-gnarled tracks more suitable for a gravel or mountain bike. Holkham Park is on National Cycle Network (NCN) Route 1, and those who arrive by bike receive a discounted entry to the hall when it is open.

On your bikes!
1. From the cycle hire or car park, follow the road towards the boating lake, passing the back of Holkham Hall. Follow the road as it turns left towards the bottom of the lake. Take the right fork to continue around the lake, and after 200m turn right through the trees.

2. Follow the grassy farm tracks up the west side of the lake, past the Church of St Withburga, and then around the top of the lake. Near the Coke Monument, turn right on to the gravel-topped path through the woods; take care when crossing the road near the north gate where you may encounter traffic heading for the park's car parks. When the track bends to meet another estate driveway, continue straight on, on the track.

3. Continue on for approximately 1 mile before turning right towards the Great Barn. At the Great Barn, turn left to follow the lane down towards The Avenue. At The Avenue, you may want to detour by turning left on to The Avenue, and proceeding through the southern gate to see the Triumphal Arch. Otherwise, cross The Avenue, and turn right at the T-junction.

4. After 1/2 mile, turn right. At the crossroads, turn left and follow The Avenue, past the Obelisk that aligns with the centre of the house, back to Holkham Hall.

Refreshments: Pub and cafes in Holkham Park.
Bike hire and repairs: At start. Hire, servicing and repairs at Wells Bike Hire, Wells-next-the-Sea.
Public transport and bike links: Cromer station, 22 miles away. Norwich station, 37 miles away on NCN 1 (largely off-road). Frequent buses to Holkham Hall from Cromer, Fakenham and King's Lynn.
Parking: Paid parking at Holkham Hall.
Maps and guides: OS Landranger 132, Explorer 251.
Website: *www.holkham.co.uk*

Start/finish
Holkham Hall, near Wells-next-the-Sea (52.9512, 0.8086, TF 888430)

Distance
7 miles/11km.

Category
Estate roads, gravel paths, grassy tracks.

Other facilities

Ride 27 Peddars Way: Great Massingham to Fring

Start
Junction of Mad Dog Lane and Greengate Lane, Great Massingham (52.7752, 0.6552, TF 792230)

Finish
Fring Road, north-west of Fring (52.8900, 0.5663, TF 727356)

Distance
9 miles/15km.

Category
Grass-topped farm tracks, occasional concrete and tarmac lanes.

Other facilities

The Peddars Way follows the route of a Roman (or possibly older) road from Knettishall Heath to the Norfolk coast. Although primarily a pedestrian trail, the Way can be cycled except from the start to Bridgham Heath, between South and North Pickenham, between Fring and Ringstead and the final section just south of Holme next the Sea. The Way forms part of the Peddars Way and Norfolk Coast Path, and is clearly waymarked with acorn signposts. Between Great Massingham and Fring, the Way largely follows grass-topped farm tracks, which may be rutted and muddy. Although this might be tackled on a touring bike with suitable tyres, it is probably best suited to a gravel or hybrid bike.

On your bikes!

1. Follow Greengate Lane for $^1/_2$ mile and turn right on to the Peddars Way. After 2 miles, take care when crossing the often-busy A148 main road. The route follows a minor road for 200m to Harpley Dams cottages where it rejoins farm tracks.

2. After 2.5 miles, you pass the late Bronze Age barrow at Anmer Minque. Continue on the Peddars Way for another 4 miles, crossing three more minor roads to reach Fring Road, between Fring and Sedgeford; the Peddars Way is a footpath north of this road.

Refreshments: Pub and cafe in Great Massingham. Pub in Sedgeford, 1.5 miles from finish.
Bike hire and repairs: None en route, although Wheel Travel Cycle Hire will deliver daily hire bikes.
Public transport and bike links: Not well-served by public transport: King's Lynn station, 12 miles from start.
Parking: Limited on-street parking at Great Massingham, Harpley.
Maps and guides: OS Landranger 132, Explorer 250.
Website: www.nationaltrail.co.uk/en_GB/trails/peddars-way-and-norfolk-coast-path

Sandringham Estate Ride 28

Sandringham House has been a favourite royal country retreat since the mid-nineteenth century, and this trail allows you to enjoy the pleasant, wooded country estate. Like Windsor Great Park (p70), the roads through the royal estate are not entirely traffic-free. You may encounter cars en route to the car parks or campsite and some estate and local traffic, however this should be light and slow-moving. On roads or well-surfaced trails, this route is suitable for any bike, although those wishing to explore the estate's woodland trails might prefer a gravel bike. Alternatively, road cyclists might enjoy extending their route to Dersingham with its pretty village pub; the North Norfolk coast is also within easy reach (seven miles).

On your bikes!

1. From the Sandringham Visitor Centre, follow Scotch Belt towards the Norwich Gates, turning left on to the road signed 'Sandringham Parking'. Continue past the parking to reach Princess Drive, a traffic-free lane that curves through woodland.

2. At the end of Princess Drive, turn right on to Folly Hill, named for the ornate hunting lodge that you now pass. Take care when crossing the Queen Elizabeth Way main road, where you may encounter fast traffic. Continue straight on through the Edinburgh Plantation, past the car park.

3. Turn right at the Old Rectory, just before Wood Farm, Prince Philip's retirement cottage for the last years of his life. As you pass through Wolferton, you will also go by the now unused railway station that the royals once used to reach Sandringham.

4. Turn right at the T-junction and follow the estate road back to the car park, again continuing straight ahead. Take care again when crossing Queen Elizabeth Way, and continue straight on, on Double Lodges Road. At the crossroads, turn left on to Donkey Pond Hill; be aware that you might encounter motorhomes or cars towing caravans en route to the estate campsite here. At the junction with Scotch Belt, turn right to return to the visitor centre.

Refreshments: Cafe and restaurant at start. The Feathers, Dersingham.
Bike hire and repairs: None en route, although Wheel Travel Cycle Hire will deliver daily hire bikes.
Public transport and bike links: Hourly bus services from King's Lynn and Hunstanton. King's Lynn station, 8 miles away. National Cycle Network (NCN) 1 (on- and off-road) links Sandringham to King's Lynn.
Parking: Paid parking at North car park, 400m from start and West car park, 100m from start.
Maps and guides: OS Landranger 132, Explorer 250.
Website: www.sandringhamestate.co.uk

Start/finish
Sandringham Visitor Centre, Sandringham (52.8298, 0.5062, TF 689288)

Distance
5 miles/8km.

Category
Estate roads, gravel tracks.

Other facilities

Index

A

Alban Way: Hatfield to St Albans	116
Alice Holt Forest	63
Alton Water	156
Ashridge Estate	110
Ashwell Street Byway	132
Ayot Greenway	115

B

Basingstoke Canal: Fleet to the canal centre at Mytchett	65
Basingstoke Canal: Mytchett Visitor Centre to Byfleet	80
Basingstoke Canal: Odiham to Fleet	64
Bedgebury Forest	39
Bewl Water, Lamberhurst	38
Black Park	106
Blackwater Valley	66
Blickling Estate	170
Brandon Country Park	162
Brighton Promenade	29
Bure Valley Path, The	165
Bushy Park	85

C

Centurion Way, Chichester	22
Cheesefoot Head	58
Chelmer and Blackwater Navigation, Maldon	148
Christmas Common to Stonor	73
Clacton-on-Sea to Frinton-on-Sea	147
Clay Way, The	126
Colchester to Wivenhoe	153
Cole Green Way	117
Crab and Winkle Way: Canterbury to Whitstable	45
Cuckoo Trail	33

D

Deers Leap Park	34
Ditchling Beacon on the South Downs Way	30
Downs Link: Bramber to Old Shoreham	28
Downs Link: Bramley to Cranleigh	25
Downs Link: Cranleigh south to Slinfold	26
Downs Link: Southwater to Bramber	27

E

E2 and the Gog Magog Hills	136
Ebury Way: Rickmansworth to West Watford	88
Egrets Way: Monk's House to Newhaven	31
Epping Forest	100

F

Fen Drayton	134
Flitch Way: Braintree to Little Dunmow	152
Flitch Way: Great Dunmow to Start Hill	151
Forest Way, east of East Grinstead	36
Friston Forest	32

G

Grafham Water	133
Grand Union Canal: Hemel Hempstead to Tring Reservoir	112
Grand Union Canal: Milton Keynes to Cosgrove	124
Grand Union Canal: Milton Keynes to Leighton Buzzard	118
Grand Union Canal: north of Denham Country Park	87
Great Stour Way, The	44
Greenwich to Erith alongside the Thames	94
Grim's Dyke, Colchester	154

H

Haddenham Horseshoe	139
Hadleigh Country Park	146
Hatfield Forest	150
Hayling Billy Cycle Trail	54
Heartwood Forest	114
Holkham Park	171
Horton Country Park	84
Hurtwood, The	24
Hyde Park	93
Hythe Seafront	43

I

Icknield Way Trail: Princes Risborough to Wendover	108
Ickworth	161
Ingrebourne Hill Bike Park	98

J

John Bunyan Trail, Bedford	128
Jubilee River Trail	71
Judges Ride	72

K

Kennet & Avon Canal through Newbury	62
Kennet & Avon Canal: Reading to Thatcham	68

Index

L

Lee Navigation: Hertford to Waltham Abbey	103
Lee Navigation: Waltham Abbey to Islington	102
Letchworth Greenway, The	130
Limehouse Basin to Westminster	95
Little Ouse Path	164
Look Out, The, Bracknell Forest/Swinley Forest	67

M

Marriott's Way: Norwich to Reepham	166
Medway Towpath, The	41
Meon Valley Trail	57
Milton Keynes to Winslow	119
Milton Keynes: Ouse Valley Trail	120
Milton Keynes: Willen Lake and Caldecotte Lake	122
Mottisfont Abbey	59

N

New Forest, Hampshire	53
Newport to Cowes Cycleway, Isle of Wight	52
Newport to Sandown, Isle of Wight	51
Nickey Line: Harpenden to Hemel Hempstead	113
Norbury Park: Leatherhead	81
North Downs Way: Lenham to Charing	42

O

Osterley Park and House	89
Oxford Canal: Heyford to Oxford	77
Oyster Bay Trail, The: Whitstable to Hampton Pier	46

P

Pages Wood	99
Peddars Way: Great Massingham to Fring	172
Peterborough and Ferry Meadows Country Park	140
Phoenix Trail: Thame to Princes Risborough	76

Q

Queen Elizabeth Country Park, Petersfield	56
Queen Elizabeth Olympic Park	96

R

Rainham Marshes	97
Reading, along the Thames to Sonning	69
Rendlesham Forest	158
River Can in Chelmsford	149
Rye Harbour Nature Reserve Loop	40

S

Sandringham Estate	173
Slough Arm Grand Union Canal, east of Slough	86
Southend-on-Sea	145
Staunton Country Park	55

T

Tamsin Trail, Richmond	90
Tennyson Trail, Isle of Wight	50
Test Way, Stockbridge	60
Thames at Tilbury	144
Thames through Oxford	74
Thames Towpath: Putney Bridge to Weybridge	91
Thetford Forest	163
Trimley Marshes	157
Tudor Trail: Tonbridge to Penshurst Place	37

U

University Way (Bedford to Sandy), The	129

V

Valley Walk, Sudbury	160
Viking Coastal Trail, The: Reculver to Margate	47
Viking Trail	159

W

Wandle Trail	92
Waterbeach to Cambridge along the River Cam	137
Watership Down	61
Weavers' Way: Aylsham to North Walsham	169
Weavers' Way: Stalham to Bengate	168
Wendover Woods	107
Wey Navigation: Godalming to Guildford	23
Wey Navigation: Weybridge to Pyrford Lock	82
Wicken Fen	138
Wimpole Estate	135
Windsor Great Park	70
Worth Way, west of East Grinstead	35

Vertebrate Publishing
Britain's best adventure books

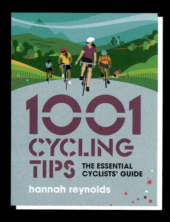

Available from bookshops or direct.
Sign up to our newsletter to save 25%
www.adventurebooks.com